# THE LIFE AND CAREER OF P.A. MCHUGH A NORTH CONNACHT POLITICIAN 1859–1909

*A Footsoldier of the Party*

# Maynooth Studies in Local History

GENERAL EDITOR Raymond Gillespie

This pamphlet is one of eight new additions to the Maynooth Studies in Local History series in 1999. Like their twenty predecessors, most are based on theses submitted for the M.A. in Local History at National University of Ireland, Maynooth. The pamphlets are not concerned primarily with the portrayal of the history of 'particular places'. All are local in their focus but that localisation is determined not by administrative boundaries but rather the limits of the experience of everyday life in the regions of Ireland over time. In some of these works the local experience is of a single individual while in others social, occupational or religious groups form the primary focus of enquiry.

The results of these enquiries into the shaping of local societies in the past emphasises, again, the diversity of the Irish historical experience. Ranging across problems of economic disaster, political transformation, rural unrest and religious tension, these works show how such problems were grounded in the realities of everyday life in local communities. The responses to such challenges varied from region to region, each place coping with problems in its own way, determined by its historical evolution and contemporary constraints.

The result of such investigations can only increase our awareness of the complexity of Ireland's historical evolution. Each work, in its own right, is also a significant contribution to our understanding of how specific Irish communities have developed in all their richness and diversity. In all, they demonstrate the vibrancy and challenging nature of local history.

*Maynooth Studies in Local History: Number 23*

# The Life and Career of P.A. McHugh A north Connacht politician, 1859–1909

## *A Footsoldier of the Party*

Íde Ní Liatháin

IRISH ACADEMIC PRESS
DUBLIN • PORTLAND, OR

First published in 1999 by
IRISH ACADEMIC PRESS
44, Northumberland Road, Dublin 4, Ireland
*and in the United States of America by*
IRISH ACADEMIC PRESS
c/o ISBS, 5804 NE Hassalo Street, Portland, OR 97213.

website: www.iap.ie



**British Library Cataloguing in Publication Data**
Liathain, Ide Ni
The Life and Cover of P.A. McHugh, 1859–1904: A footsoldier of the party – (Maynooth studies in local history; 23)
1. McHugh, P. A. 2. Politicians – Ireland – Biography 3. Ireland – Politics and government – 1837–1901
I. Title
941. 7'12'081

ISBN 0716526778

**Library of Congress Cataloging-in-Publication Data**
Ní Liatháin. Íde.
The Life and Career of P.A. McHugh, 1859–1909: A footsoldier of the party/Íde Ní Liatháin.
p. cm. — (Maynooth studies in local history: no. 23)
Originally presented as author's thesis (M.A.)—National University of Ireland. Maynooth, 1998.
Includes bibliographical references (p. ).
ISBN 0–7165–2677–8 (pbk.)
1. McHugh, P.A., 1859–1909. 2. Politicians—Ireland—Connacht Biography. 3. Connacht (Ireland) — Politics and government. 4. Ireland—Politics and government—1837–1901. 5. Ireland—Politics and government—1901–1910.
I. Title. II. Series.
DA958. M38N5 1999
941.7'1081'092—dc21
[B]

99–29351
CIP



Typeset in 10 pt on 12 pt Bembo by
Carrigboy Typesetting Services, County Cork
Printed by ColourBooks Ltd, Dublin

# Contents



FIGURES

# Acknowledgements

My thanks are due to many people who have helped me during the course of my research: the staff of the National Library of Ireland, the National Archives; Sligo County Library; and the library of St. Patrick's College Drumcondra. I would also like to record my thanks to Most Rev. Dr. Francis J. MacKiernan, former bishop of Kilmore, for providing information from the archives of St. Patrick's College, Cavan.

I am deeply indebted to Dr. Mary Ann Lyons and Dr. Raymond Gillespie of the Department of History in Maynooth, for their help and encouragement during the M.A. course. My thanks also to Professor Vincent Comerford, head of the department.

I would like to thank my employers, South Dublin County Council, for financial and other assistance; my colleagues in the library service, especially the staff of Clondalkin library, who ensured I got to my lectures on time! Finally, thanks to my family for their support and infinite patience.

# Introduction

This is a study of P.A. McHugh, M.P. for Leitrim North from 1892 to 1906, and for Sligo North from 1906 until his death in 1909. He was a member of the Irish parliamentary party which represented Irish national aspirations in the 'Imperial Parliament' at Westminster until they were obliterated by Sinn Féin in the general election of 1918. Prior to being elected to parliament, he had been a prominent local organiser and supporter of Parnell's party machine in Sligo. His newspaper the *Sligo Champion* was very much part of the machine, as he used it as propaganda vehicle for the party and of course, for his own activities.

A local history study usually examines a particular place or locality with well-defined boundaries, rather than an individual. By studying the career of a local politician, the impact of national events on a particular place, and the level of political participation can be gauged. McHugh was more associated with his adopted town of Sligo, than with his native Leitrim, although he was a very influential figure in both counties. Therefore, his activities were not confined to a specific place. Although he spent most of his life living in Sligo town, the dominance of agrarian issues in late nineteenth-century Ireland, and the interdependence of town and county, meant that rural concerns dominated his political career.

The earlier part of McHugh's career in politics was dominated by Parnell, and his legacy has been extensively studied by historians. The Parliamentary Party during and after Parnell's leadership has been the subject of two masterly works by Conor Cruise O'Brien and F.S.L. Lyons, both of which are invaluable for a study of the Irish nationalist movement in the period under discussion.[1] As well as chronicling the party's fortunes, both books examine the membership of the party, and how the political machinery operated. Many individuals who were prominent in the party remain largely unknown, although they were to dominate Irish politics long after Parnell's downfall. T.M. Healy has only recently been the subject of a major biography, and William O'Brien's importance was unknown for many years. T.C. Harrington and Thomas Sexton have been neglected completely, and the main study of John Redmond was published over sixty years ago.[2] The suggestion could be made that the parliamentarians were written out of Irish history by the generation who defeated them at the polls, and who went on to found the new state. Irish political biography however, is a relatively new genre, and renewed interest is being shown in the post-Parnell period, which had been perceived as a 'featureless valley between the commanding chain of the Rising and the solitary enigmatic peak of Parnell'.[3] If the 'lieutenants' and leaders have been relatively forgotten, it is no wonder that the footsoldiers like McHugh remain in obscurity, although Michael Davitt described him as 'a nationalist with a record second to that of few men in the popular movement'.[4] It is only very recently, with the advent of county histories that local politics has been examined in detail and, as yet, neither Sligo nor Leitrim have been the subject of a major county history. The role and influence of the press in a society which was becoming more literate is another topic which needs to be researched, although a recent study has redressed this gap in historical research.[5]

McHugh did not enjoy the longevity of many his colleagues, and he did not write any memoirs which would assist a study of his life. Neither does there seem to be any collection of his correspondence or any other papers. Some letters of his can be found among the papers of major figures such as William O'Brien in N.U.I. Cork, and John Redmond. In the absence of such material, I have relied heavily on the *Sligo Champion* as a source for his activities, and those of the local organisations with which he was involved. This dependence on his own newspaper does create problems, as one naturally gets a one-sided viewpoint. Other sources include police reports, which give the 'official' view of McHugh.

The first chapter looks at his background and examines his initial involvement in local politics and his rise to prominence in Sligo town. The second chapter deals with the period when he consolidated his position in Sligo, the Parnell split in the county, and McHugh's election to Westminster in 1892. The final chapter studies the apogee of his career, when he was involved with the new County Councils, the United Irish League, and when he also faced a number of legal challenges.

# The Making of a Local Politician

Patrick Aloysius McHugh, or P.A. as he was to be known, was born in March 1859 to Peter McHugh and Mary Keany, in the townland of Annagh near the village of Glenfarne, County Leitrim.[1] Glenfarne is situated in north Leitrim on the road from Manorhamilton to Enniskillen, close to the Cavan and Fermanagh borders. His father was a tenant farmer who leased fifty acres of mountainy land from John Massy of Hermitage, County Limerick, who owned 24,751 acres in Leitrim.[2] P.A. was educated at a local primary school and in 1872 he was sent to St. Patrick's College, Cavan, as a boarder. Like all other Roman Catholic secondary schools in Ireland, St. Patrick's was a private institution. In 1855 when the Royal Commission on Endowed Schools visited the college, then called St. Augustine's, the fees for boarders were £6 per quarter, with an entrance fee of one guinea.[3] Rev. John O'Reilly, a teacher at the school, informed the Commission that the school's pupils were drawn from 'the middle classes; from the farming class and the respectable class of Catholics in this County'.[4] The proportion of the population attending secondary schools at this time was tiny. In 1871, only 1,200 Roman Catholics in the whole of Connacht were attending 'superior' schools, which were schools teaching a foreign language, and in 1881, this figure had fallen to 880 for the province.[5] St. Patrick's was the diocesan seminary for the diocese of Kilmore, and McHugh was enrolled as a clerical student. He studied both philosophy and theology to second level, but in June 1878 he left the college, or, perhaps more accurately, he was asked to leave, as the College Council decided that his tendency to disobey the rules rendered him unfit for a clerical career.[6] In 1879, he went to Paris for a year.

McHugh returned to a country that was in the grip of a severe agricultural depression, which particularly affected the west of Ireland, where densely populated areas still depended heavily on the potato crop for their livelihood. In Mayo, Michael Davitt became involved in agitation protesting against the plight of tenant farmers. He persuaded Parnell, who at that time was a leading member of the Irish Parliamentary Party, to join the campaign. The Irish National Land League was established, and it was the first political mass movement since the days of O'Connell. The movement grew quickly and local branches were formed all over the country. The League encouraged passive resistance to evictions and discouraged 'landgrabbers', who would occupy farms from which a tenant had been evicted.

The method used by the League to enforce its authority was the boycott. It was not new, but it now became widespread, especially as enunciated by

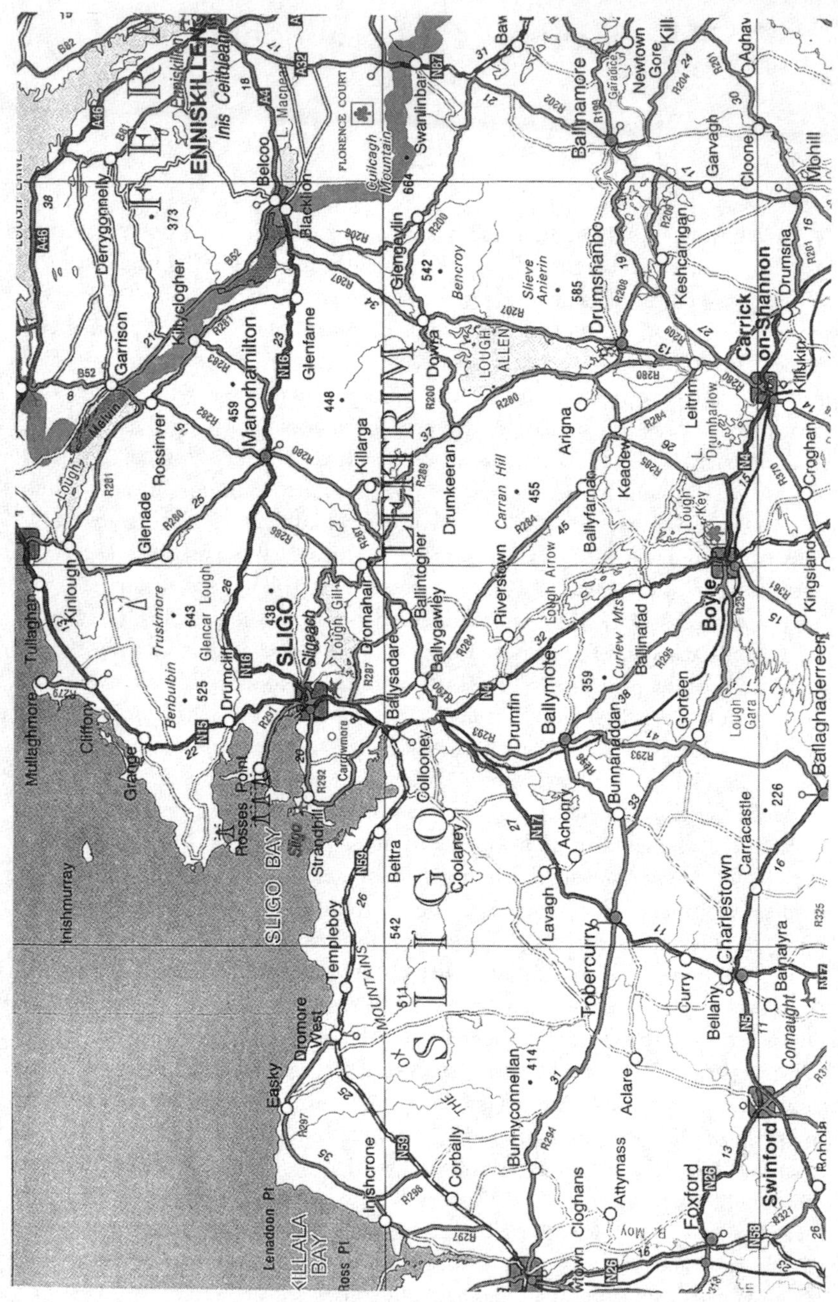


1. Map of Sligo and Leitrim, based on Ordnance Survey Ireland by permission of the Government Permit No. 6846.

Parnell in a celebrated speech in Ennis in 1880, when he advised his audience on dealing with 'grabbers' 'by isolating him from the rest of his kind as if he were a leper of old, you must show him your detestation of the crime he has committed'.[7] Others who were targetted were land agents, bailiffs and anyone who had any contact with the victim. Local 'courts' were held to arbitrate in disputes, where all sides got a hearing. Anyone who broke the rules of the League was summoned by the local branch to explain their transgression. Members were assisted in various ways, whether through food and clothing, legal help, or the building of 'league huts' for evicted tenants. Large public demonstrations were held to articulate the demands of the League. 'Indignation' meetings were also held to protest against evictions or 'grabbers'. The government responded by introducing special legislation which gave wide-ranging powers to the courts and to the lord lieutenant. Many activists were imprisoned, and the League was proclaimed in October 1881. The agitation was then organised by the Ladies Land League, led by Anna Parnell, sister of Charles, who was now leader of the Irish party in Westminster, and an inmate of Kilmainham gaol. When he was released he quickly put an end to the ladies' League.

The Land League politicised a whole generation of Irishmen, giving them valuable experience of political agitation and organisation. It was to be the model for local political organisations in the future, and it was retrospectively viewed as a true nationalist movement which embodied the spirit of unity and purpose of the time.[8]

Despite the political ferment in which he found the country on his return from Paris, McHugh had a more mundane matter to occupy his attention: that of earning his living. He secured a teaching post in Athlone, and then moved to Sligo to teach in the College of the Immaculate Conception, known as Summerhill College. In November 1880 he married Mary Harte of Sligo, and although later he was to stress his humble background, his father, the bride's father and himself are all described as 'gentlemen' on the marriage certificate.[9] His wife died in 1894, and in 1900, he married her sister Katie, although at the time English law forbade a marriage between a man and his sister-in-law.

Summerhill was a second level or 'intermediate' school. Legislation had been introduced in 1878 which established public examinations, and schools were funded by the state on the basis of the results obtained. Secondary school teachers were not required to have any specific training for the job, and their conditions of employment lagged behind those of national school teachers. There was no set salary and no pension. Their tenure of posts was uncertain, and as most Catholic teachers taught in schools run by the church, laymen could only play a subordinate role. In 1878 an observer remarked that second level teaching was 'about the worst mode of obtaining a livelihood open to a man of intelligence'.[10]

Sligo town, strategically placed between Ulster and Connacht, was founded by the Normans in the thirteenth century. In 1612, the town was created a borough by James I, and large numbers of Scottish and English settlers came to live there. In the first half of the nineteenth century Sligo endured the great cholera epidemic of 1832, which devastated the town, and the Great Famine of the 1840s.[11] The town recovered however, and in 1881 the population was 10,808, and it was the most important seaport on the north-west coast.[12] Sligo had undergone somewhat of a building boom in the previous decades. The Italianate town hall had been built in 1866, the Roman Catholic cathedral for the diocese of Elphin was completed in 1874, and finally the assize courts with its 150 foot frontage was unveiled in 1879.[13] Weekly butter and corn markets were held and exports went through the port to Liverpool and Glasgow. These cities were also served by passenger ships, especially Glasgow, a frequent destination for emigrants and seasonal workers from the north-west. The railway reached Sligo in 1862, connecting the town with Dublin, and with towns in between such as Boyle, Carrick-on Shannon, Longford and Mullingar. In 1881, the line to Enniskillen was opened, connecting the town to Belfast.[14] These improvements in transport and communications helped to develop the trade and industry of the town. Thus, Sligo had the appearance of a bustling, prosperous town. Affluent businessmen included Henry Lyons, who owned a large drapery establishment, and the Pollexfens, shipping agents and millers, who were to become famous through their connection to the Yeats family. These merchant and trading families were looked down upon by the aristocratic landed gentry such as the Gore-Booths of Lissadell, the Coopers of Markree castle, and the Wynnes of Hazelwood. John Butler Yeats was later to complain of the attitude towards his wife's family, the Pollexfens 'because they were engaged in business they were not fit company'.[15]

Teaching was to be McHugh's profession until July 1885, when he became proprietor and editor of the *Sligo Champion* newspaper. He retained an interest in education, especially in the working conditions of teachers, and he also served as an examiner for the Intermediate examinations for several years. The *Champion* or *Sligo News* had been founded in 1836, by Edward Verdon, at the request of the Liberals of Sligo, who wanted to counter-act the influence of the Tory *Sligo Journal*.[16] Verdon declared his editorial policy in the first edition, published on 4 June 1836

> We come forward in a country where the voice of liberty has been stifled, and where the sacred rights and privileges of the subject have been violated, to advocate the cause of a long oppressed people, to be the fruitful, the unflinching, and, we trust, the invincible *champion* of civil and religious liberty.[17]

By 1851, the circulation was 10,000 per week.[18] On Verdon's death in 1858, the paper was published by Edward Gayer, who was active in the Land League. He was the chairman of the Sligo branch of the League, and presided over a large demonstration in the town which was addressed by Michael Davitt, John Dillon and Thomas Sexton, who was one of Sligo's M.P.s.[19] He served as a councillor on Sligo Corporation. Although he was a supporter of the Land League, and was charged with publishing a threatening notice, a charge which was withdrawn, he criticised its more radical leanings. In an editorial in July 1880, he condemned the 'violent language' used at a League meeting in Irishtown in County Mayo, where the speaker had poured scorn on constitutional agitation. He advised people to follow the advice of the priests, and to avoid 'illegality'.[20]

When he died in 1884, he was succeeded for a brief period by Tadhg ('Thady') Kilgannon, who declared that the paper was 'the exponent of Catholicity and Nationality in the West of Ireland'.[21] By this time the *Sligo Journal* had ceased to exist, but two other newspapers had appeared in the 1850s. The *Sligo Chronicle*, founded in 1850, was owned by the Sedley brothers, who were both solicitors and members of Sligo Corporation. Its policy was to 'advocate

*2.* P.A. McHugh
courtesy of the *Sligo Champion*

*moderately* conservative views'.[22] In 1855, the *Sligo Independent* was published by the Gillmor brothers. The newspaper was to be 'Conservative' in politics although the editor was anxious to stress that this did not mean exclusion for 'the wronged and the oppressed, from the peasant to the peer.'[23]

The first edition under McHugh's ownership appeared on 25 July 1885. He promised that he would continue the policies of his predecessors, 'to make this paper the exponent of the principles of the Irish National League, and to uphold the policy of the Irish Parliamentary Party, whose confidence and support the *Sligo Champion* has always possessed'. He also declared that he felt that it was his 'sacred duty' to give 'voice and tongue' to the feelings and sympathies of his co-religionists.[24] He quickly became involved in the public life of the town. He now became prominent in the Sligo Borough branch of the Irish National League, and also became active in the Gaelic Athletic Association, whose first branch in the county was established in Sligo town.

The Irish National League was established in October 1882, to replace the Land League. The National League however, differed from the Land League in its structure and aims. It was created as an electoral machine for the Irish Parliamentary Party, and was intended by Parnell to be subordinate to the party. Although Parnell was chairman of the Land League, it had maintained its independence, as many of its activists, coming from a fenian background, distrusted electoral politics and constitutional agitation.

The political emphasis of the Irish National League was to be firmly on the attainment of home rule, with land reform in second place. The League was tightly controlled by the parliamentarians, despite its constitution, which allowed for local representation on the central council. Out of a total of forty-eight members, thirty-two were to be elected at county conventions made up of local delegates. The remaining sixteen members of the council were to be selected by the Irish Parliamentary Party. This central council however, was never constituted, and control of the League remained with the organising committee of the founding conference, which was presided over by Parnell, and dominated by members of parliament. Delegates from local branches, which were usually formed on a parish basis, together with the local Roman Catholic clergy, attended county conventions to selct the party candidates for elections. In reality however, nominations were controlled by a small group, consisting of men such as Sexton, Healy and William O'Brien. They and other senior members of the party attended the conventions, which were usually held in private, to ensure that the chosen candidate was selected. These conventions contrasted with earlier selection processes, where local groups of clergy and laity met to choose a candidate. For the 1885 general election, all candidates had to sign a pledge requiring them to sit, act and vote with the party. Remarkably, there seemed to be very little criticism or rebellion against the centralised, often autocratic character of the party and the League, which must be due in no small way to the charisma and authority of Parnell.[25]

At the general election of 1880, Sligo returned Thomas Sexton, who was then virtually unknown, but he became one of Parnell's 'lieutenants', and one of the leading orators of the Parliamentary Party. Also returned was Denis M. O'Conor, a Catholic aristocrat.[26] O'Conor was one of the 'intransigent Whigs' who would not serve under Parnell's leadership and he left the party in January 1881.[27]

The Irish National League grew slowly in Sligo. It was not until 1884 that the organisation began its growth in the county, and there was no branch in the town until the spring of 1885.[28] Using lists of active members in newspaper reports for both the Land League and the National League, one can see a certain degree of continuity in personnel, but not as much as would be expected. Of the twenty-eight delegates who attended a meeting in Sligo in November 1880 to hear Sexton, Dillon and Davitt, only nine became active, and therefore identifiable in later years.[29]

McHugh used his newspaper as a propaganda vehicle for the Irish National League, exhorting 'all who wish to be regarded as true Nationalists' to join up. He saw it almost as a duty for every parish and townland to be part of the League; when new branches were formed he saw them as having 'fallen into line with the other districts of the county'. At times his enthusiasm got the better of him 'The Irish National League is the greatest organization which ever bound together the children of the Irish Race', but such flamboyant language was quite typical of the time.[30] He came in for criticism from the former Land Leaguer James Daly, his 'contemporary' of the *Connaught Telegraph*, who called the *Sligo Champion* 'the subsidized organ of the great dictator Parnell', but P.A. declared himself to be proud of this allegation.[31]

Political power in Sligo was vested in the corporation. The borough had been a parliamentary constituency until 1870, when after a Royal Commission of enquiry, it was disfranchised because of persistent corruption. The corporation consisted of six aldermen and eighteen councillors elected from three wards: north, east and west. The electorate was limited to men who occupied property with a rateable valuation of £5 per annum. Councillors had to own property worth £1,000, or occupy a house with a poor law valuation of £25. Elections were held annually for one-third of the councillors, and every three years for the aldermen.[32] The mayor was elected annually and in Sligo from 1867, he was chosen

> alternately from those holding Conservative and Liberal opinions, so that in future each side of the house shall do their best to induce a cordial good feeling in the Corporation, and by sinking their political differences, unite their best efforts for the moral and material improvement of the Borough[33]

The mayor was by his office, the chief magistrate of the borough, and chaired the petty sessions courts. From 1854 he received a salary, which in 1888, the first year McHugh held the office, was £200.[34]

The corporation was limited in its powers, which were strictly defined by legislation. The councillors could pass bye laws, and they dealt with public lighting, water and sewage supply, the town's markets, and street paving and cleaning. They were limited in their powers of raising finance. Although municipal representation consisted solely of property owners, there does not seem to be any evidence of a movement to reform the system.

Most criticism was reserved for the administration of the county, which was in the control of the grand jury and the poor law boards. The grand jury was selected by the high sheriff, who was appointed annually by the lord lieutenant from among the leading landowners in the county, and they made decisions on expenditure relating to roads and buildings. They also served as jurors in criminal cases held at the assize courts in Sligo.

The poor law boards of guardians consisted of both elected and *ex-officio* members; the latter constituted one-half of the membership of the board. They were chosen from local magistrates. Elected guardians had to occupy property valued in the region of £20, and the voters were confined to those whose residences had a valuation of at least £4.[35] However, for the poor law elections, there was a system of multiple voting, which gave more votes to those who paid higher poor rates. Votes could also be accumulated by large property owners in their different roles as owners and occupiers, which could bring their total voting power up to twelve votes. Ballots were signed by voter, therefore their choice was a matter of public record.[36] The county was divided into poor law unions, each with its own boards, elcted from electoral divisions. County Sligo consisted of five poor law unions, two of which crossed the county border: Sligo, Tubbercurry, Dromore West, Boyle and Ballyshannon. The functions of the boards included the maintenance of the workhouse, medical care, registration of births and deaths, water supply and the housing of rural labourers. By the 1880s, poor law boards were becoming less dominated by large landlords, and were being targetted by nationalists as power bases. When McHugh was first nominated as a councillor, he reminded his audience that 'Mr. Parnell is more than anxious that all public boards should be made as representative of the aspirations of the Irish people as possible'.[37] In the case of poor law boards, he agreed that the system needed reform, but he argued that some minor changes could be made if 'men of the right stamp', that is, members of the Irish National League were elected.[38] The poor law boards were to remain objects of nationalist criticism because of their undemocratic nature.

In his editorials, McHugh commented on both national and local issues. He criticised the corporation for its lack of economy and its inefficiency, themes which he was to reiterate through the years. In his opinion, the poor law system fostered 'idleness' among those dependent on it, and the Sligo board was seen as failing in its obligations to the labourers. He urged young men to join the GAA, and he became involved in the Sligo House League, which was a branch of a nationwide movement to achieve for town tenants what the Land League had for their rural counterparts. On national issues he gave unswerving support to Parnell. After Gladstone's first home rule bill was defeated in 1886, he advised nationalists to await 'the instructions which the great Leader of the Irish Party will issue'.[39] Parnell was seen as the inspiration of the national movement, and it was the duty of the Irish people to be loyal to him. Even when Parnell insisted on the nomination of Captain O'Shea as the candidate for Galway in 1886, though he would not sign the party pledge, McHugh glossed over the 'misunderstanding' between Parnell and members of the party. When O'Shea voted against the home rule bill, it was merely seen as proof of Parnell's humanity, that even the 'Irish Chief' was fallible.[40] McHugh professed admiration for Gladstone, 'the greatest minister that England has ever seen', and he praised the home rule bill as a 'just, generous, and comprehensive measure', although he acknowledged its defects, such as the power of veto which the two chambers of the proposed native parliament had over each other.[41] He also criticised the fact that the Royal Irish Constabulary was to remain under the control of Westminster for several years. He did not contemplate the defeat of the bill, although later, when it fell on the second reading, his opinion was that even if passed by the house of commons, the bill would not have got through the house of lords.[42] His optimistic reaction in April was a common one in Ireland, unconnected with the possible future of the bill: 'At last a great statesman and a great party had been brought to embody Irish aspirations in legislative form'.[43] After the disappointing result in Westminster, and the subsequent dissolution of parliament, he advised against a violent reaction, and the influence of the 'extremists', who 'have all along ridiculed the constitutional agitation of the Irish party . . . Violence, intolerance and religious bigotry must be left exclusively to the Orangemen of the North who have always monopolised these problems in Ireland'.[44]

McHugh saw his newspaper as a vital part of the nationalist movement, which informed and advised a certain constituency. No attempt was made to represent any other viewpoint, and none would have been expected by his readers. To modern readers, who have become used to expect polictical impartiality from newspapers, the whole-hearted support of a particular viewpoint seems strange, and at times, comical, but McHugh was writing in a different age, for people who depended entirely on newspapers for information about the distant world at Westminster, and even local politics, in which the majority of them did not participate. Parnell knew the value of the press. In 1881, he established *United Ireland*, with William O'Brien as its enthusiastic editor, because he felt the the *Freeman's Journal* did not give him unconditional support.

McHugh's constituency, as well as being nationalists, were also Roman Catholics. One of his constant criticisms of the poor law boards, was their appointments of Protestant doctors, matrons and nurses, in a county which was overwhelmingly Roman Catholic. As chairman of the Irish National

League in Sligo, he proposed adjourning meetings of the branch during the holding of a religious mission in the town.[45]

McHugh became a member of the committee of the Sligo Borough branch of the Irish National League in September 1885. A list of the committee and membership of the branch is available in Sligo County Library.[46] The document is very valuable, as it not only gives the names and addresses of the members, but also, in the majority of cases, their occupations. This information can be used to examine the type of people who constituted what would now be called the 'grass roots' of a large political organisation. The 139 members on the list were all men; the 'ladies' of the town were not involved in politics, and only occasionally attended political meetings. Only ten of those on the list are not given an occupation. The four branch officers of the branch were the chairman, who was Thomas Sexton, MP, the vice-chairman was Patrick O'Connor, a grocer and shirt dealer. The deputy vice-chairman was John J. Keenan, a pawnbroker and 'clothier', and the secretary was 'Thady' Kilgannon, former editor of the *Sligo Champion*, now a 'printer, stationer and photographer'. The sixteen strong committee was later reduced to fifteen; the town was divided into five areas, who chose three members each.

The biggest occupational group among the membership were grocers and spirit merchants. Of the 129 members for whom an occupation is given, twenty belong to this group, some combining dual roles as grocers and publicans. Other groups, such as victuallers and butter merchants, bring the combined number of food based occupations to thirty-seven. The next largest grouping of occupations could be described as tradesmen and artisans; they include carpenters, coopers and even hairdressers. Grocers' and hardware assistants account for fifteen of the members, and 'labourers' for five. Other occupations included a reporter, an editor, two law clerks and only one farmer.

Six of the members were already involved in local politics: five town councillors and one alderman, all of whom were in the grocery and spirits trade, although Alderman Richard McDonagh also operated a shipping agency. This predominance of shopkeepers of various types is also seen among the membership of the Land League, in which they often assumed the leading role in their locality. Indeed, of twenty-eight members of the Sligo branch of the Land League already mentioned, eleven can be identified as grocers.[47] Shops and public houses were places where people gathered and met one another. However, artisans and tradesmen seemed to have had a bigger representation in the Irish National League in Sligo than in Clark's study of the Land League.[48] Perhaps this is because Sligo was a major town, with less of a rural population than smaller towns. The National League therefore, was representative of a large cross-section of the town, although, with only five labourers as members, it can be concluded that it was predominantly an organisation of the middle and lower middle classes. For example, there were no domestic servants among the membership. There are no members of the clergy mentioned; they were usually considered honorary members, and were always invited to selection conventions.

The members met regularly although, at times, the attendance was not large enough for important discussions. Sometimes, the meetings could get rather too lively; McHugh complained in an editorial about the manner in which the Sligo branch conducted its meetings. Members at meetings should be 'dignified' and interruptions by 'a few obnoxious individuals' should not be allowed, as this exposed their cause to the ridicule of its enemies. He obviously came under attack for his reporting of the League's proceedings, as he was forced to defend their veracity several times, and he refused to censor his reports.[49] He proposed rules for the conduct of meetings, under which members could be expelled if they did not obey the chairman. Later rules governed entry to the branch, which was through a committee member. If a committee member missed three consecutive meetings, he was to be replaced.[50] The first member to be expelled was Martin Waters, a publican, who was accused of 'land grabbing' by the Grange branch in north Sligo. After an investigation, he was expelled, and his name does not even appear on the list of members of the branch.[51] The second member to be excluded was John Reid, whose expulsion was proposed by McHugh for his 'disorderly and insubordinate conduct'. His friends protested that his only crime had been to ask why the branch reports were not sent to *United Ireland*, but they were shouted down.[52]

In 1885 the major task for the League members was to prepare for the election convention, which was held to select the two candidates for the general election for the new constituencies of Sligo North and Sligo South. The Redistribution of Seats Act 1885, had divided the county into two separate parliamentary divisions, each returning one member. Another important statute, the Representation of the People Act 1884, had dramatically increased the numbers of those entitled to vote.[53] Prior to this legislation, electors had to satisfy certain property qualifications. The Act of 1884 enfranchised all adult male householders who had paid their rates, and who had resided at their address for twelve months. In Sligo, the electorate increased from 3,258 in 1884 to 18,033 in 1885.[54] The 'mud-cabin' vote was to prove a staunch ally of Parnell, who initially viewed the measure somewhat coolly.

The Sligo branch received instructions from the headquarters of the Irish National League advising them to select men who by their 'integrity, judgement, and disposition to work in a spirit of loyalty and harmony with their colleagues, are capable of forming an honest, intelligent, and united party'. The method suggested to find such sterling men, was a convention 'acting in conjunction with Mr. Parnell and his colleagues'.[55] Later it was announced that Sexton was to be joined on the ballot paper by Peter Macdonald, 'an intimate friend of Mr. Parnell', who had 'the approval of the Bishops of Elphin and Achonry'. In a letter to the branch, Sexton suggested that Sligo follow other counties who had already held conventions, such as Wicklow and Meath, and stage a 'public' meeting after the selection process.[56] The branch requested shopkeepers to close at 3 p.m. on the great day, to ensure as big an attendance as possible. The four delegates elected to represent the Sligo branch were Owen Dolan TC, Alderman McDonagh, McHugh and Bernard Collery.[57]

The convention was preceded by the conferring of the freedom of the borough on Thomas Sexton, only the second man to receive the honour.[58] McHugh addressed him at the railway station, and led the torchlight procession through the town. Delegates from thirty-five branches from around the county attended, and large numbers of the Roman Catholic clergy. The proceedings were held in private, so there is no record of any dissension when two delegates proposed P.N. Fitzgerald as a candidate for Sligo South. The report merely states that he withdrew his candidacy when Sexton was proposed. Resolutions were proposed by McHugh who was acting as one of four secretaries. These resolutions praised Parnell and his party, expressed demands for a 'native parliament', the reduction of landlords' power, supported home industries, labourers, and condemned 'landgrabbing'. The speakers included Joseph Biggar MP, one of the better known members of the party, and Michael Conway MP for Leitrim North.[59]

Thus, the convention followed the formula by which most other county conventions were governed. The delegates, guided carefully by a leading member of the parliamentary party, had endorsed the party's candidates, who then signed the party pledge. Alexander Perceval and Col John Ffolliot, the candidates who opposed Macdonald and Sexton, were dismissed by McHugh as 'the descendants of some Cromwellian horseboys'.[60] Both nationalist candidates were returned with very comfortable majorities.[61]

With the convention over, the branch members had completed one of their major tasks. Another of their functions was to raise finance to fund elections; in 1880 Sexton's campaign had cost £251, and O'Conor's the immense sum of £1,441.[62] Although affluent candidates were sought by the party, some MPs were unable to support themselves at Westminster, and they received funding from the party; they were the first members of parliament to receive a salary. The Sligo branch contributed to the 'central branch', and also collected monies for special collections.

Although the political programme of the Irish National League stressed the primary aim of achieving home rule, the rural branches were still preoccupied with agrarian matters, especially as yet another economic depression, beginning in 1885, led to falling agricultural prices. Gladstone's proposed land bill of 1886 received a lukewarm wecome from the borough branch. The members however, were loath to be critical of the 'Grand Old Man', and passed a resolution in his favour. Town merchants buying farms, and outbidding farmers was a contentious subject, but McHugh defended the townsmen, as long as they did not buy a farm from which the occupier had been evicted.[63] This issue caused friction between the members, as some of them did farm land outside the town. John Connolly TC offered to rid himself of his farm if it was found that he had violated the rules of the League.[64] When a member complained that he had lost a corporation contract to a firm outside the county, he was told that a 'petty private grievance' was not the business of the National League.[65]

The branches in rural Sligo were based on the Roman Catholic parish or half-parish, and meetings were usually held after mass on Sundays, often in the 'chapel yard'. Rural branches often asked the parish priest to act as their president, and he would often chair the meetings. This organisational basis followed the example of the Land League, and they were in fact, reactivated branches of the old League. By checking newspaper reports of members of both organisations, it can be seen that there was a more marked continuity in the leadership than in Sligo town.[66] What the country branches had in common with the town was the predominance of grocers and shopkeepers among those who were officers of their local branch. They were on committees in the larger towns of Tubbercurry and Collooney, and also in villages such as Bunnanadden.[67]

The careers of two of the most prominent rural activists are worth examining as examples of how such men came to be leaders in their own communities. Nicholas H. Devine was a shopkeeper in Tubbercurry who had been involved in politics since O'Connell's repeal movement. He was a delegate to the Land League convention held in September 1881, and in 1882 he was one of the many activists imprisoned under Forster's 'coercion' laws. He was also to serve for many years as a member of the Tubbercurry board of guardians.[68] In 1883 he 'withdrew' from contesting a by-election in Sligo 'after consultations with the National Leaders'.[69] John O'Dowd was a shopkeeper in the south Sligo village of Bunnanadden. He had become involved with the Land League shortly after his return from a stay in the United States, and like Devine, had served a prison sentence for his activities.[70] In 1887, he was elected as a poor law guardian for the Owenmore division of Tubbercurry Union.[71] Thus, the two men had impeccable nationalist credentials for assuming the leadership of their local areas, and their occupations allowed them both the opportunity to become well-known figures, and the time to pursue their political careers.

As the economic depression deepened, tenant farmers were unable to pay their rents, and consequently, evictions became imminent. The Sooey branch complained of the 'unjust' demands of the landlords, and the members helped to build a house for a farmer who had been evicted by Colonel Cooper of Markree.[72] The Templeboy branch had written to the landlords in the vicinity requesting rent reductions, but had only received one positive answer. In Gurteen, a branch of the National League was formed as a response to the eviction of a local widow, whose land was 'grabbed' by a shopkeeper.[73] The activities of the branches were, therefore, rooted in the agrarian concerns of their members. There was some interaction between town and county, as members of the town branch often went to meetings held by the rural branches.

While home rule was being actively pursued by the Irish party in Westminster, agrarian agitation was not encouraged by its leaders. With the defeat of the home rule bill in June 1886, and the resounding defeat of the Liberals in the subsequent general election in July, confidence in constitutional methods faltered. Parnell attempted to warn the house of commons of the impending disaster in Ireland, and he introduced a Tenants' Relief Bill to assist tenants who were in financial straits. This was rejected by the Conservative majority in the house. With the autumn rents looming, the party leadership feared an outbreak of renewed agitation, and they were determined to control it. In October 1886 a 'plan of campaign' was launched in *United Ireland*. The plan suggested that tenants on an estate offer the landlord what they considered a reasonable rent, and if he refused, they were to pay money into a central fund, which would be used to help any evicted tenants. The plan was controlled by Parnell's 'lieutenants', in particular William O'Brien, John Dillon and Tim Harrington, secretary of the Irish National League. Parnell did not take part in the agitation, which marked a new phase in the land war.

The Sligo town members were not directly affected by the renewed agitation, but they showed enthusiasm for the struggle. Even before the plan was officially announced, McHugh and others attended a demonstration at Gurteen, which was held to protest against a local 'grabber'. The meeting was addressed by William O'Brien, Jasper Tully, editor of the *Roscommon Herald*, and McHugh. O'Brien advised the farmers to take communal action and demand rent reductions. McHugh spoke in terms of a war against landlords and rent.[74]

McHugh was embarking on his career as a public figure in Sligo. In October, he was nominated by the League to contest the west ward in the municipal elections. Michael Milmoe TC called him 'the father of the National League in Sligo'. McHugh modestly replied that he had not the least ambition for the position.[75] His opponent was the outgoing councillor, the solicitor W.R. Fenton, whom he defeated by just one vote.[76]

The Irish National League had organised a demonstration in the town which was to be addressed by William O'Brien. The meeting was to be held in support of Jasper Tully, who was to be prosecuted at the winter assizes for publishing certain National League reports, along with tenants from the notorious Clanricarde estate in Woodford, County Galway. The demonstration was banned by the local magistrates on the instructions of the Chief Secretary Hicks Beach, on the grounds that it would intimidate the jurors.[77] McHugh condemned the action of the authorities in strong language: 'The liberty of the people in the exercise of their constitutional right to publicly discuss the action of their rulers, is to be throttled'.[78]

Despite the proclamation, O'Brien, Tully and Peter Macdonald MP arrived on the evening prior to the demonstration, and held a meeting in the town hall. Extra police and army units had to be brought to the town from several counties, and some of the crowd, including Nicholas Devine were batoned. It was decided to hold meetings throughout the county the following day, and McHugh and Tully were to remain in town. O'Brien addressed meetings in Ballymote, Collooney and Riverstown. In Sligo, Dr. Tanner MP held a 'mobile' meeting, which started in town and moved to a football pitch, and ended by being addressed from a boat in Lough Gill.[79]

Over the next few weeks, McHugh attacked 'jury-packing' at the Sligo assizes. He accused the crown officials of securing Protestant juries in the trial of the Woodford 'traversers', who were charged with obstructing and assaulting bailiffs who were attempting to evict tenants

> It is one of the boasted principles of the British constitution that subjects tried on grave charges can be convicted only by the verdict of their peers. That right has been during the week, denied by the Crown to the Woodford prisoners. They have been tried not by their peers, but by men diametrically opposed to them in religious and political sentiments.[80]

In the same month he received a summons to attend Magherow petty sessions court on charges arising from his speech in Gurteen, that he 'solicited and incited people to conspire to disturb the peace of the Queen'. The offence was compounded by the fact that the speech was published in the *Sligo Champion*. If he did not give sureties as to his future behaviour, he could face up to six months in jail. The presence on the bench of two magistrates from the borough who were members of the National League, caused some disagreement as to whether they had a right to be there, but they refused to budge. The magistrates could not agree, and McHugh was acquitted and enjoyed a triumphant return home, with the usual accompaniments of bands and bonfires.[81]

In the new year, 1887, agitation continued and demonstrations were held in Templeboy and Geevagh.[82] In February, Sexton, elected for two constituencies, resigned his seat in Sligo South, and elected to retain his seat in Belfast West. His replacement, Edward J. Kennedy, a member of Dublin corporation, was recommended by Parnell, and was accepted without question. In March, Arthur Balfour was appointed chief secretary for Ireland. He was to gain the epithet 'bloody' for his determined approach to suppressing unrest in Ireland. In July, the Criminal Law and Procedure (Ireland ) Act became law. Under the terms of the act, special measures could be taken in areas 'proclaimed' by the lord lieutenant. Resident magistrates could question people under oath, and anyone suspected of involvement in inducing others to boycott or to withhold rent, would be tried by a non-jury court. In the case of a jury trial, the venue could be changed.[83]

Sligo was one of the counties proclaimed under the act, and the Irish National League quickly organised a convention in protest.[84] McHugh chaired the meeting of delegates, and regretted the absence of the clergy, which was due to the presence in Sligo of Monsignor Persico, the envoy sent by Pope Leo XIII to enquire into conditions in Ireland. He declared that the object of the meeting, which was addressed by Michael Davitt, was to protest against 'coercion', and to show the world that they were not 'a land of slaves'.[85] In his capacity as a town councillor, he met Monsignor Persico, who also met Catholic groups such as the Society of St.Vincent de Paul, and landowners like Sir Henry Gore-Booth and Lord de Freyne. While the agitation continued, the more mundane business of the League was carried out. This included selecting candidates for the minicipal elections, arbitrating on an eviction case, and establishing a fund to assist the widow of Edward Gayer.[86]

At the close of the year, McHugh was nominated for the position of mayor, although he had only served one year as a councillor, and had not been a very regular attender at corporation meetings. Contrary to custom and practice, the Conservative councillors opposed his nomination, and refused to second the proposal. A poll was called for, and McHugh won by twelve votes to nine. He protested that although he was regarded as an 'extreme politician', he had never proposed a 'political' resolution at corporation meetings.[87]

Thus, although living a mere seven years in the town, and not yet thirty years of age, McHugh had become a substantial local politician. The ownership of the only 'nationalist' paper in Sligo undoubtedly helped him to articulate and influence the political views of his fellow townsmen, an opportunity not enjoyed by his colleagues in the Irish National League. His success was also due to his energy and to his involvement with local groups such as the GAA and the Catholic Literary Society, which brought him into contact with people not directly involved with politics.

# Towards a Wider Stage

1888 was to prove a year of mixed fortunes for McHugh. In January he was installed as mayor; he promised to 'guard the interests of the rate-payers', but also to express opinions on national issues and 'to give to the National Cause the influence attaching to the office with which I am invested'.[1] By virtue of his office he became involved in a range of local activities. The mayor was the chief magistrate of the borough and chaired the local petty sessions court, which usually dealt with offences such as drunkeness, trespass and other minor offences. He was an *ex-officio* member of the Harbour Board, whose members were drawn from the wealthier merchants of the town. He was also entitled to attend meetings of the board of governors of the Sligo and Leitrim lunatic asylum. The mayor was expected to be involved in the social and philanthropic activities of the town. He was the chief organiser of the 'Galgorm Castle' fund, which was established to support the families of six men drowned when their ship was wrecked in Sligo bay.[2] As the leading Roman Catholic citizen, he was a member of a number of fund-raising committees.

There were other duties, which in contemporary terms might be described as 'junkets'. He was invited to Dublin for the conferring of the freedom of Dublin city on John Morley, who had briefly served as chief secretary for Ireland in Gladstone's ministry. He enjoyed an 'at home' in Dublin's Mansion House with Sexton, who was then lord mayor of the city, and accompanied the Harbour Board members to London, where they appealed for a treasury grant in order to deepen the harbour. While in London McHugh appeared as a witness before the house of commons select committee on Sunday closing. After assuring the committee that he had no connection with the drinks trade, he gave his opinion that he favoured the opening of public houses on Sundays, rather than interfere with the right of a 'working man' to have a glass of beer. He warned that drinking at home would lead to a greater consumption of spirits, and recommended the abolition of illicit 'shebeens'.[3]

In the spring of 1888, he contested the Sligo union poor law elections, and was returned for the Lakeview division. He publicly named the only Roman Catholic who had voted for his opponent, and dismissed him as a 'grabber'.[4] When the new board met to elect a chairman, McHugh decided to oppose Col Cooper, the long-standing incumbent. He told Cooper that he opposed him on the grounds that: 'you are a landlord' . . . 'you belong to a class which has rendered workhouses a necessity in this country . . .'[5] He denounced the exclusive employment of Protestants in the workhouse posts, such as the master, the matron and the doctor, when the majority of the inmates were Roman Catholics. Predictably, with the aid of the *ex-officio* votes, Col Cooper was re-elected. McHugh's remarks generated some controversy, and he was accused by a League member from St. John's of making 'sectarian remarks', but most branches applauded his 'manly action' in contesting the chairmanship.[6]

League members throughout the country were to receive a devastating blow in late April when the results of the mission of Monsignor Persico from the pope to investigate the state of Ireland became public. In a papal decree or rescript, it was declared that 'in disputes between letters and holders of farms and lands', activities such as boycotting and the plan of campaign were unlawful, and that 'a rent fixed by mutual consent, cannot' . . . 'be reduced at the arbitrary will of the tenant alone'.[7] In an overwhelmingly Roman Catholic country like Ireland, where bishops and priests were regarded as being leaders in both spiritual and material affairs, the decree seemed to deliver a hammer blow to the aspirations of those involved in the agrarian struggle. McHugh, although declaring that silence was the most prudent course of action, asserted that the decree 'was founded on falsehood', and that the morality of boycotting was 'indisputable'.[8] When the Sligo branch met to discuss the issue, a resolution was passed which regretted the pope's views, and staunchly asserted that in politics, the members would follow Mr. Parnell, 'in whose wisdom and rectitude we have entire confidence', and not 'a body of Roman cardinals evidently misinformed as to the political condition of this country'.[9] This was quite a remarkable statement when one considers that the bishops had not yet made a public pronouncement on the decree. The Roman Catholic members of the Parliamentary Party did not give their answer until 18 May, when they repudiated the right of the pope 'to interfere with the Irish people in the management of their political agitation'.[10] The plan and boycotting were to continue.

The next matter to claim the attention of League members was the resignation of E.J. Kennedy, MP for Sligo South. McHugh decided that Parnell would probably prefer if the constituency picked its own representative, but accepted the right of the party to 'veto' a candidate.[11] It would appear that there were rumblings of discontent among some branches, and that McHugh was aware of this. Three south Sligo branches, Collooney, Riverstown and Sooey, nominated McHugh as Kennedy's successor. In a letter to the *Champion*, Michael Davitt recommended Dadabhai Naorje for the vacancy; in nominating him, Sligo would strike a blow for Indian freedom.[12] Davitt had proposed Naorje for an Irish seat back in 1883, but Parnell had decided against the idea.[13] A convention was fixed for 3 June at Ballymote, although the practice of holding conventions had not been continued after the 1885 general election.

At the convention McHugh was duly selected, although Naorje did receive a nomination which was then withdrawn.[14] Ominously, the Achonry branch objected to the convention, which it felt had been called without the approval of the central branch, and at a time when the clergy, 'the chief officers of branches', could not be present.[15] Unfortunately for McHugh, his selection was ignored by the decision makers in the party, and at the end of the month, *United Ireland* announced that 'Mr. Edmund Leamy, at the unanimous request of Mr. Parnell and the Irish Party, has considered to re-enter political life'.[16] Although he must have felt some degree of disappointment, McHugh did not complain publicly, and praised Leamy's work in defending those charged with offences under the Crimes Act. Leamy was elected unopposed, and his nominators and assentors included many of those who had attended the Ballymote convention.[17] The public display of acceptance and obedience to Parnell's decision reveals the absolute control which he held over the League.

Deprived of being placed on the national stage, McHugh was to be thrust into the limelight when he was arrested for publishing an article regarding land-grabbing in Templeboy, in which he intimidated 'certain persons in consequence of their having done what they had a legal right to do, and incited others to use intimidation'.[18] When the case was heard, a further charge of intimidation against Michael Coffey was added.[19] Coffey had occupied a farm in Gurteen from which a widow had been evicted. He had been boycotted by the local branch for some time. When he had brought a malicious injury claim to the grand jury, McHugh had written in an editorial that Coffey 'must continue to live the barren and friendless life of a social leper.'[20] This editorial was quoted in the charges, and McHugh received the maximum sentence of six months.[21] An appeal was immediately lodged, and at a demonstration in the town, he declared himself willing to do the same again, and denied that he had incited to violence, which he felt was bad for 'the cause'.[22] While the appeal was pending, McHugh did not show any signs of lessening his activities or toning down his views. He continued to attend the petty sessions court, the board of guardians and the county board of the GAA, of which he was president. He attacked what he considered as local injustices, such as the appointment of a Protestant doctor by the Riverstown Dispensary committee, although the Catholic applicant had acted as a *locum tenens* for some time.[23]

Judge O'Connor Morris confirmed the sentence, describing boycotting as 'one of the most grievous offences against the body politic', and McHugh was brought to Derry gaol to serve his sentence.[24] During a six month period, only eight other people in Sligo were prosecuted in the 'coercion' courts, and the charges were withdrawn, except in the case of James Mahon, who received two months with hard labour for assaulting a policeman. Sligo was one of the quieter counties, with only nine cases appearing in court, in comparison with Leitrim's thirty-three, and Clare's eighty-seven.[25] The corporation passed a vote of sympathy with McHugh, and the League organised a testimonial which attracted subscribers from the USA and Australia, realising a sum of £400.[26] The prisoner's health gave cause for alarm in the new year when it was reported that he was a patient in the infirmary with bronchitis, which was 'more than likely to prove fatal'.[27]

This gloomy prediction proved exaggerated, however, and in March he was re-elected to the Sligo board of guardians in his absence. His release in May was the occasion of widespread demonstrations at every railway station along his route back to Sligo. In the town itself, the GAA band led a torchlight procession to the market cross, where McHugh informed the crowd that before he went to prison, he was 'a moderate law-abiding subject to the Queen', but that on his release he had become 'a rebel against the administration of English law in this country'. He again defended the use of boycotting against land grabbers, 'who try to enrich themselves at the expense of the interests of the community'.[28] That week he accompanied the mayor John Connolly to London, where an address from the corporation was presented to Parnell, who replied in a 'brilliant and stirring speech'.[29] In June, the new GAA club in Bunnanadden named their team the 'P.A. McHugh's', which was indeed an honour, as most clubs used the names of nationally known leaders such as Parnell, Dillon and Davitt.[30] He could be regarded, therefore, as a major political figure in his own county, whose reputation was greatly enhanced by his incarceration in Derry gaol.

His position as a poor law guardian was threatened when his defeated opponent, John Hunter challenged the result of the election, and the Local Government Board informed McHugh that an enquiry would take place.[31] The objection centred on whether McHugh fulfilled the rateable qualification, and there seemed to be some confusion as to whether McHugh or his wife's aunt was the rateable occupier.[32] The inspector found in favour of Hunter, and although McHugh attempted to contest the election, his nomination was rejected by the returning officer.[33] Before his ejection from the boardroom, he continued to criticise the inefficient and 'lazy' rate collectors, whom he contrasted with those in Tubbercurry union, which had a nationalist majority on the board.[34]

Although McHugh declared that unlike other organisations which tended to lose some of their initial energy, the Irish National League was as powerful as ever, he complained that committee members were not attending meetings of the branch, and that the barony of Tireragh, in the west of the county, had no branches of the League. An 'organising committee' was established in north Sligo to re-energise the movement which, inevitably was chaired by McHugh. A similar committee had already been established in south Sligo, and in several parliamentary constituencies throughout the country. Moribund branches, such as Geevagh, were visited by the committee and 're-organised'. Their lack of action was seen as a temporary aberration from their distinguished nationalist past.[35]

On new year's day 1890, McHugh was summonsed on charges that he incited intimidation towards Jones Taaffe McDonagh and John Killoran, who had taken two evicted farms at Sooey. Once again, the publishing of branch reports from Sooey and other areas which warned traders against supplying goods to the two men, was part of the indictment.[36] McHugh's editorial comments on the two cases were also brought to the attention of the court, and despite the fact that Killoran denied that he had been intimidated, the magistrates sentenced the defendant to four months imprisonment, and to give sureties for good behaviour, or spend a further two months in prison.[37] The appeal was heard shortly afterwards, once again before Judge O'Connor Morris, who described McHugh as a man 'of cultivation and a man of extreme ability'. He again condemned boycotting, but in confirming the sentence, dismissed the two months in default of £100 bail, because he felt that the boycott had been ineffective.[38] Even his political opponents in the *Sligo Chronicle* admired his courage and tenacity, but could not resist the jibe that even his own party 'seem inclined to hold aloof from him'.[39]

McHugh was not the only member of the fourth estate to be prosecuted. Several editors, who were also MPs, were also to suffer the 'plank bed' of the coercion laws, despite an assurance from Balfour that he would not interfere with the freedom of the press. These men included T.D. Sullivan, MP, of the *Kerry Sentinel*, Edward Walsh of the *Wexford People*, and Alderman Hooper, MP, of the *Cork Herald*.[40]

For his second term of imprisonment, McHugh was sent to Tullamore, which was known as 'Balfour's Bastille', because of the rigid enforcement of the prison rules by the governor. Its most famous ex-inmate was John Mandeville, a farmer who along with William O'Brien was tried for activities connected with the plan of campaign. The demonstration called for the day of the trial ended in the infamous 'Mitchelstown Massacre', in which three people were killed by the police. Mandeville received a sentence of two months, and died in July 1888, seven months after his release from Tullamore. The verdict of the inquest jury blamed his death on the brutal regime in the prison. The Dublin Castle authorities did not want to create more martyrs, and instructed prison officials to pay attention to the health of the coercion prisoners.[41] Shortly after his arrival in Tullamore, McHugh was suffering from a cold, and questions were asked in the house of commons by Peter Macdonald regarding his treatment.[42] J.A. Macauley, who had taken over as the editor in McHugh's absence, was, together with John McLoughlin, secretary of the Sooey branch of the Irish National League, charged with intimidation and criminal conspiracy, and both served six weeks in prison.[43] When he was released, McHugh once again received a hero's welcome, and again he gave a stirring speech to the assembled crowd. He denounced the coercion regime as 'an outrage upon the principles of constitutional government', and if Irish people submitted to it, their allies, the English Liberals, would 'think us cowards, unworthy of freedom'.[44]

His second term of imprisonment led to his removal from the post of superintendent for the Intermediate examinations.[45] He also came to the attention of the Special Crime Branch of the Royal Irish Constabulary. A 'biography' of him was sent to Dublin Castle outlining his activities and his previous convictions. He is described as 'a man of considerable literary abilities, and is looked to by the nationalists as their leader in this County'.[46] The police seemed to be under the impression that he was the 'County Centre' of the Irish Republican Brotherhood, and were correct in stating that the 'North Sligo Organizing Committee' had collapsed since his imprisonment. There does not seem to be any evidence however, to link McHugh with the 'extreme' nationalists, and in his public pronouncements, he always deplored the use of violence. Having come to the notice of the Royal Irish Constabulary, he was placed on their 'B' list of suspects, who were to be 'ciphered'; his movements were to be watched, and Dublin Castle was to be kept informed.[47] 'A' list suspects were national leaders such as William O'Brien, who were to be 'shadowed'.

The damp weather in the summer of 1890, and reports of potato blight led to grave concerns for the coming winter. As it became obvious that crop failure was widespread, the boards of guardians in Sligo and Tubbercurry appealed for government intervention, and suggested the building of light railways to provide employment. Balfour had introduced a scheme for constructing such railways in 1889, as part of his 'conciliation' policy in Ireland. McHugh considered the situation as being as bad as the catastrophic years of 1845 and 1879: 'The Irish people are again face to face with ruin, misery and starvation'.[48] He accompanied Leamy and Macdonald on their visit to Sligo to ascertain the extent of the blight, and to meet with local leaders. Meetings were held all over the county, and each group wanted any proposed railway to run through their own area. The situation was grave, and revealed that the west of Ireland was still at the mercy of the potato crop for its existence. Although Sligo was not as badly affected as Mayo, many people were faced with disaster.

The disaster in the west was soon overshadowed by events in a London divorce court involving Parnell and his mistress, Mrs. O'Shea. Her husband, Captain O'Shea, had filed a divorce petition in December 1889, citing Parnell as co-respondent, but the case was not heard until mid-November 1890. The Irish leader was at the height of his popularity, having been vindicated by the Special Commission established to investigate allegations that he was linked with terrorist activities. The 'union of hearts' between the Irish Parliamentary Party and the Liberals seemed secure, and by-election results seemed to indicate a defeat for the Tories in the next general election. Several of Parnell's 'lieutenants' had known about the liaison since the Galway city by-election in 1886, when O'Shea had been nominated as the party's candidate, almost leading to a split in the ranks. The divorce case was not defended by either Mrs. O'Shea or Parnell, and the one-sided evidence revealed a sordid story of deceit and betrayal. The granting of a decree to Captain O'Shea was inevitable.

The Irish Parliamentary Party in the following days was in a state of confusion and uncertainty, but at a public meeting in Dublin, attended by many leading MPs, confidence in Parnell's leadership was renewed. A telegram was received from Dillon and O'Brien, who had fled to the USA to avoid yet another trial, pledging their support. Michael Davitt was the only political figure in nationalist Ireland who called on Parnell to resign, as he correctly foresaw that Gladstone and the Liberals would not agree to Parnell's continued leadership.[49]

In Sligo, as in most of the country, when news of the impending court case was received, it was seen as a continuation of the vendetta being pursued by the London *Times*, which had published the notorious forgeries. A special meeting of the corporation passed a resolution expressing confidence in Parnell, and denounced 'the system of persecution' which had dogged him in the past, and sympathised with him in the 'threatened renewal of similar nefarious attacks'.[50] When the details of the divorce proceedings became known, the *Sligo Champion* reserved its anger for the 'Pharisees of the Tory and Unionist Press', who had disregarded the cardinal rule of 'honourable men', which allowed for comment on a man's public and political conduct, but which 'strictly prohibits comment or criticism upon him in his capacity as a private individual'.[51] He praised Parnell's record and his 'priceless services' to Ireland, and declared that his personal life was as irrelevant to Irish politics as 'the colour of his hair or the cut of his coat'.[52] This was of course, exactly how Parnell himself viewed the whole matter.

By the following week however, the political landscape had changed. On 25 November, the Irish Party held its annual meeting to elect the chairman of the party, and as on every occasion since Parnell had attained the leadership in 1880, he was unanimously re-elected. The following day however, the press published a letter written by Gladstone to John Morley, in which he stated that the continued leadership of Parnell would 'render my retention of the leadership of the Liberal party, based as it has been mainly upon the prosecution of the Irish cause, almost a nullity'.[53] Thus, the 'union of hearts' with the Liberals which had been the foundation for Parnell's policy since 1886, was now endangered by its own architect, and consequently, home rule itself was threatened. The letter had not been intended for publication, but Gladstone, under pressure from non-conformist public opinion in England, which strongly condemned Parnell, felt it would force the Irish Party to repudiate its leader. The letter served its purpose, and a further meeting of the party was fixed for 1 December.

In Sligo, McHugh rounded on those MPs who had called for the meeting and blamed the 'flood of cant and hypocrisy' from the British press for their weakening resolve. He condemned their 'unparalleled ingratitude and treachery' for bowing to Gladstone's threatened resignation. He admitted that it would be a 'great misfortune' if the 'Grand Old Man' was to retire, but in his view, it would be worse to lose Parnell before the completion of his 'gigantic task'. He continued to profess his loyalty to Parnell, while acknowledging that he had 'committed a great wrong', which in England was usually regarded as 'a mere pecadillo'. He called on the Irish people to be loyal to their leader 'as long as he is willing to lead them'.[54] In the same issue of the *Sligo Champion*, there was a report of a demonstration in Drumkeeran, County Leitrim, attended by Michael Conway, MP for Leitrim North. In his speech Conway declared that the only remedy for the current misery in the county was legislative independence, and he advised tenant farmers to provide for their families before they paid any rent. At no time at the meeting, which was attended by several priests, was Parnell's name mentioned. The paper also printed a branch report from Sooey, which seemed to be one of the few active Irish National League branches at this time. The branch confirmed its loyalty to Parnell.

The same day, 29 November 1890, Parnell issued his 'Manifesto to the Irish People', in which he now stressed the absolute independence of the Irish Party from the Liberals in particular, and the English parties in general. He also gave details of Gladstone's alleged future plans for Irish home rule, which he condemned. He concluded that postponing home rule would be 'preferable to a compromise of our national rights'.[55] The tone of the manifesto provoked Dillon and O'Brien, still in America, to condemn Parnell for endangering any future alliance with Gladstone. The Irish Party assembled in committee room fifteen in Westminster for their tortuous meeting which was to last for six days. In the same week, the standing committee of the Irish hierarchy finally pronounced on the issue, and inevitably they declared Parnell to be an unsuitable leader of the Irish party.

McHugh lamented that once again:

> fatal dissension which has ever dashed the cup from the country's lips when hope seemed brightest . . . men who fought side by side during the last ten years, are at each other's throats, a grief to their friends, a glory and gratification to their enemies[56]

He seemed to favour the idea that the Irish constituencies should be consulted by their members, but this proposal had already been defeated at Westminster. He still refrained from denouncing Parnell:

> we are not among those who are prepared to turn and rend him at the bidding of British Pharisees. Mr. Parnell has done more for Ireland than any man who ever laboured in her cause, more than O'Connell, more than Butt. Before we cast from us, before we spurn from us, for a moral transgression, this illustrious benefactor of our race, we should reflect and hesitate.[57]

He continued to castigate the Irish MPs for their desertion of Parnell, after initially supporting him in public in Dublin and Westminster, and praised those who stood by him. He also commended Parnell's policy of independence at Westminster: 'the Irish party must be independent or contemptible. Tories and

Liberals are all the same to the people of Ireland, who may expect no measure of Home Government except what is wrung from either party'.[58] McHugh now however, expressed the opinion that Parnell should have resigned after the divorce case. The hierarchy's statement on the crisis was published in full, but McHugh made no comment on its content. The speeches made by Leamy and Conway, the two local members who aligned themselves with Parnell, were also published, and of the four Irish National League reports, two, Calry and Magherow, contained expressions of confidence in Parnell, while Keash and Grange seemed to be divided on the issue.

By the following week the split had occurred in the Parliamentary Party, with Justin McCarthy the vice-chairman, leading the majority of the party out of committee room fifteen. McHugh saw it as 'a day of shame and sorrow and tribulation for Ireland', and he refused to take sides, declaring that each side had erred. He called for a national convention to be held, which could attempt to heal the rift, and he thought Parnell's future rested with Dillon and O'Brien. The Manorhamilton board of guardians had passed a resolution expressing approval of the majority of the Parliamentary Party, and condemning Michael Conway for supporting Parnell. McHugh berated them for the second part of their resolution:

> What has Mr. Conway done? He has stood by his leader. His action may have been mistaken, but who can deny that it was an act to which any man with a noble and chivalrous nature would have been impelled?[59]

Some local branches of the Irish National League, such as Highwood and Keash, now came out against Parnell, while others like Collooney and Sooey did not mention him in their reports.

The first opportunity to test public reaction in Ireland on the issue of Parnell's involvement in the divorce suit arose when the writ for the Kilkenny North by-election was moved. Polling took place on 22 December. The exchanges were bitter, and Davitt, who led the anti-Parnellite campaign, and Parnell himself, were physically assaulted. McHugh deplored such 'disgraceful' incidents, and advised people not to take any action at present, but to wait until William O'Brien had made a definite pronouncement. His attitude towards Parnell was however, hardening; he warned that the Irish people would not tolerate the present strife for very long, and that if Parnell was defeated in Kilkenny, they would attribute any continuation of the struggle on his part 'not to principle or patriotism but to personal ambition'.[60] Although his tone had changed, he was still moderate and rational, unlike Jasper Tully of the *Roscommon Herald*, who derided the tumultuous reception that Parnell received in Dublin: 'Dublin, the moral cesspool of Ireland . . . came out from its slums and brothels to welcome Mr. Parnell'.[61] More local branches of the league declared against the 'Chief'; Culfadda and Ballintogher called on Leamy to retire, while Grange and Dromore West still retained a neutral stance. A correspondent wrote from Ballymote that most people were still loyal to Parnell.

When the Parnellite candidate in Kilkenny North was defeated, McHugh saw the result as a type of national opinion poll, and called on Parnell and his followers to resign their seats and test their own constituencies. For the first time he referred to Parnell's personal life, although he had condemned others for doing so. He attributed opposition to Parnell to the fact that he was a 'convicted adulterer'.[62] He had not seen this as an issue before, and it is not clear what bought about this change in the approach he adopted. McHugh appeared to be firmly in the anti-Parnellite camp, and he asserted that most of Sligo was of the same opinion. The only League branches still supporting Parnell were Sooey and Ballyrush.

In the new year of 1891, the country awaited the outcome of the negotiations between Parnell, Dillon and O'Brien, which took place in France, as the latter two still faced arrest in Ireland. Dillon hoped to persuade Parnell to resign, by granting him some concessions which would allow him to leave public life with some dignity. When the talks broke down at the end of January, O'Brien and Dillon returned to London to face the six months imprisonment they had fled in October. The anti-Parnellite leaders began to promote a new political organisation to succeed the Irish National League, to be called the Irish National Federation, which was formally established in March 1891. During this period, McHugh concentrated on local issues, such as the distress in Tireragh, the emerging labour movement in Sligo town, and the formation of a committee, of which he was a member, to establish a club, where 'respectable' Catholic men of the town could meet.[63]

When the Boulogne negotiations broke down, McHugh resumed his attack on Parnell: 'his present mad, selfish obstinacy is ruining our chances of obtaining in the near future the legislative independence of our country'.[64] He now urged all parishes to establish branches of the Irish National Federation. The new organisation did not have much time to establish itself in the county before Sligo became the focus for the next stage in the struggle between the two factions. In mid-March, the death occurred of Peter Macdonald, the member for Sligo North, and the by-election was fixed for 2 April. The consitituency, McHugh declared, was strongly anti-Parnellite, apart from parts of Tireragh, where the local bishop, Dr. Conway of Killala, 'is not merely indifferent, but rather encourages the support of Mr. Parnell'.[65] The local newspaper the *Western People*, based in Ballina, was also Parnellite in opinion. Parnell's candidate, V.B. Dillon, a Dublin solicitor, who was a cousin of John Dillon, was referred to as a 'Whig attorney' by McHugh.[66] Although his uncle was a resident of the town, Dillon was not well-known to the voters, despite his illustrious name. His opponent was Bernard Collery, an established merchant and former mayor of the town. He was selected at a convention, which was attended by the bishops of Elphin and Achonry. Once again,

McHugh had been passed over for the glittering prize, although he did not give any hint of disappointment or bitterness. He saw Collery's selection as a triumph for local consitituency organisations, which in the past had been ignored by Parnell and Harrington, 'the autocrats of Upper O'Connell Street'.[67] He seemed to have forgotten that the inner group who had chosen candidates also included Healy, Dillon and O'Brien.

Parnell's campaign, which was concentrated on Tireragh in the west of the constituency, was not given much coverage in the *Sligo Champion*. His supporters in Sligo town were addressed by the Parnellite MPs Col Nolan, John Redmond and Luke Hayden, and they included many former members of the Irish National League, some of whom signed Dillon's nomination papers.[68] Prominent anti-Parnellites, such as Sexton and Davitt campaigned for Collery, and both sides had to endure mob violence. Parnell based himself in Ballina for the campaign, and was accompanied to a meeting in Sligo town by several of his supporters from Mayo, who seemed to act as his bodyguards. McHugh was attacked by Parnell, who called him a 'cowardly little scoundrel' who had fled when he saw his former idol.[69] He accused McHugh of having attempted to disrupt a meeting in Leitrim in 1880, at which Parnell was present, and alleged that McHugh's father was a bailiff. He later apologised for these remarks when he received a solicitor's letter on behalf of McHugh.[70]

The result was a victory for the anti-Parnellites, who polled 3,261 votes to Dillon's 2,493.[71] The turnout was quite low, especially in Sligo town, where nearly one-third of the voters stayed away from the polling booths. Many may have been unionist voters, and others may have decided to turn their backs on the two warring factions. As expected, Dillon fared best in Tireragh, where it was estimated he took three-quarters of the votes polled. Voting had been quite heavy there, especially in Easky and Enniscrone, where turnouts of over 85 per cent were recorded.[72] It would seem that the Sligo town vote had been decisive, although in the general election of the following year, towns were more likely to support Parnellites than rural areas.[73] The anti-Parnellites attributed their opponent's success in Tireragh to its geographical remoteness and political backwardness.[74] McHugh professed astonishment that so many people had voted for Parnell's candidate, and blamed the priests of the region who 'intimidated their conscientious people into voting for the adulterer', and he named those he felt responsible: the parish priest of Dromore West, the bishop's administrator in Ballina, and curates in Easky and Dromard. He also alleged that personation had been widespread, and blamed the low turnout in other areas on the complacency of anti-Parnellite voters.[75] Other recriminations followed the election, when the Parnellite mayor Thomas Connolly, was strongly criticised for not allowing Michael Davitt to use the town hall.[76]

When the dust settled after the by-election, McHugh became involved in establishing branches of the Irish National Federation around the county, although he seemed slow to become active in the Sligo town branch. From a list of seventy-seven members who subscribed to the new organisation, thirty-seven can be definitely identified as former members, indicating a high degree of continuity between the two organisations, and also the extent of anti-Parnellism in the town.[77]

It is difficult to discover who the Sligo Parnellites were and to gauge their strength as they were virtually ignored by the *Sligo Champion*, as if they did not exist. The Parnellites of Tireragh however, were neither forgiven nor forgotten. A prominent Parnellite in the area, John Clarke of Easky, was denounced as a 'grabber', a 'worthy disciple of the Elthamite adulterer', a reference to Mrs. O'Shea's house in Kent.[78] He was described as a merchant and a grazier, and it was seen as symptomatic of the area where Michael Davitt was stoned, that it would produce such a man.[79] Parnell's supporters were regarded as being on a par with the traditional enemies, the landlords. In July, the overwhelming defeat of A.J. Kettle, the Parnellite candidate in the Carlow by-election, was greeted with 'rejoicing in Sligo'.[80]

In local matters, the attention of the National Federation was directed towards raising money for a brass band, and McHugh conducted a war of words with Fr. Crofton of Cliffoney, president of the Federation branch in the parish, because the priest wished to present a local landowner, Evelyn Ashley of Classiebawn, with an address on his marriage. McHugh denounced the idea of collecting money for a 'coercionist' and 'rackrenter', and dubbed the priest a 'flunkey'.[81] In the rural branches the problem of 'grabbing' still persisted. Because of the impending general election, members were urged to ensure that they were registered to vote, and that they had paid their poor rates.

Despite the bitterness and invective which characterised McHugh's language during the spring and summer months, Parnell's death came as a profound shock, and his sorrow was genuine:

> That he was a leader of towering genius, unflinching, tenacious of purpose, resourceful, self-possessed, and far-seeing, his bitterest opponents will not deny. No man ever possessed more fully than he the confidence, the admiration and the love of the Irish race.[82]

Like many others at the time, McHugh seemed to think that Parnell's death removed any barrier to nationalist unity, and that the two sides could now be re-united. The atmosphere however, was too poisoned with hatred to allow for reconciliation. Moderates like William O'Brien were not heard, and exponents of hard-line rhetoric, of whom Tim Healy was the most vociferous, took centre stage. The extreme language of the exchanges may take the modern reader by surprise, but it gives a flavour of the mood of the country and the language of political discourse at the time. The great party which Parnell had so skillfully guided to its apogee of power in 1886, seemed to have self-destructed.

The impending general election of 1892 was to be the first nationwide contest between the two factions. The anti-Parnellites relied on the system of county conventions to select their candidates to contest the seats which were held by their opponents. They took the same form as the pre-split conventions, although there was much less centralised control, as the party was still re-grouping and attempting to resurrect the machinery of the old party. It was not until the end of May 1892, that a committee was set up to direct the election arrangements. By that time, many constituencies had already held conventions. In the week before the committee was established, the two constituencies of Leitrim held a joint convention at Drumkeeran. Conventions were usually held in the county town of Carrick-on-Shannon, but because of 'Parnellite rowdyism' in the town, it was considered safer to meet in the northern division.[83]

Delegates from all over the county attended, as well as about thirty priests and GAA members. The convention was chaired by John Roche MP, and the two candidates selected were McHugh for Leitrim North, and Jasper Tully for Leitrim South.[84] As was the custom before the split, the proceedings were held in private, and the full details were not released to the press, so it is impossible to discover whether any other names were proposed or whether there was any opposition to the two men who were selected. McHugh was proposed by Rev. James Dolan, parish priest of Drumkeeran, and seconded by John McGuinness, a poor law guardian from Manorhamilton.[85] After both men had signed the party pledge, a public meeting was held.

McHugh modestly protested that he was 'wanting in many qualities and attainments that would be desirable in your representation', but that he had one advantage, which he saw as being of supreme importance, in that he had been 'born and bred in the bogs of Leitrim', which was a barb directed at Michael Conway and Parnell's policy of selecting candidates from outside the constituency.[86] In his speech, McHugh castigated Conway for breaking the parliamentary pledge, which bound him to a decision of the majority. He considered the pledge to be vital to the success of the party, and that it had made Parnell's party 'the strongest and most effective body of Parliamentary representatives ever sent by Ireland to the English House of Commons'. He was careful however, to distinguish between Conway and those who supported him. Those on the Parnellite side were seen as gullible men, who had been led astray by Conway and the other 'pledge-breakers'. He declared that he would work for an amnesty for Irish political prisoners, the amelioration of the conditions of labourers, and the restoration of evicted tenants to their holdings.

These issues, in McHugh's opinion, were secondary to the attainment of home rule, which would lead to a more egalitarian and prosperous Ireland:

> We want a system of Government under which every man who is willing to work may be well housed, well clothed and well fed, and under which

> every man who sleeps in his bed at night may lie down with the consciousness, that he is a man and not a slave, and that, however humble he may be, he has at least a voice in the Government of his Native land.

Referring to the differences in the party which had arisen over the management of the *Freeman's Journal*, he promised that he would be 'neither a Dillonite or a Healyite', and would stand aloof from all factions. He also asserted the independence of the party from all other parties at Westminster, and vowed that if the Liberals produced a 'milk and water measure' of home rule, the party would show no hesitation in voting against them. The anti-Parnellites had been strongly criticised by their opponents for their surrender to Gladstone's ultimatum. He also defended the role of the priests in the controversy, praising them for acting 'as a bulwark between the people and their oppressors'.[87] The ideas expressed in McHugh's address were those of orthodox Irish nationalism of either camp. What was noteworthy was that he did not mention the land question, which would have been uppermost in the minds of his rural audience.

During his campaign McHugh visited most parts of the constituency, and also canvassed for Bernard Collery in north Sligo. Although he was expected to pay most of the costs himself, he applied to the election committee for £35 for 'personal expenses', which he received after forwarding a detailed account.[88] No Parnellite candidate was nominated for either Leitrim constituency and McHugh's opponent was Charles G.L. Tottenham, representing the Unionists, the name now used by the Conservatives. Tottenham was a member of a landowning family, whose mansion was quite close to McHugh's childhood home. One of the Tottenhams had been elected in 1880, but the estate had been declared bankrupt in 1885. McHugh now turned his attention to the traditional enemy. In his published election address, he again stressed his Leitrim roots, and now emphasised his humble origins: 'Leitrim men should refuse to be represented by imported frauds, or by the ignorant and worthless off shoots of a decayed and bankrupt landocracy'.[89] He now promised to advocate the compulsory sale of land to tenants, and the resolution of the turbary problem which was causing disputes in parts of the constituency. He was in favour of the abolition of the grand jury system, the *ex-officio* guardians, and plural votes in poor law elections. He had an easy victory over Tottenham, who only polled 541 votes to McHugh's 4,688.[90]

In August, McHugh and Collery left Sligo for London. At thirty-three years of age, he was ten years younger than the average age of the Irish nationalist MPs, and he was one of thirty-five new members who had no previous parliamentary experience. As a journalist, he was a member of the second largest occupational grouping among the nationalist ranks, consisting of thirteen members in 1892, demonstrating the importance placed by the leadership on the influence of the press.[91] Gladstone, now in his eighty-third year and leading his fourth ministry, had a precarious majority, which depended on the support of the Irish nationalists, made up of seventy-one anti-Parnellites, and nine Parnellites, but he was prepared to introduce a bill introducing home rule for Ireland. Hopes were high that it would be attained. After the Queen's speech and the Address, parliament was prorogued to allow Gladstone to prepare the long-awaited bill.

Parliament did not meet again until the end of January 1893, and on the second day of the session, McHugh moved the first reading of the Evicted Tenants' Bill. The bill was drawn up by members of the party, and proposed in McHugh's name. The first reading was merely a formal proposal, but during the second reading, he had to introduce the debate. Some of the evicted tenants were casualties of the demise of the plan of campaign, which had gained benefits for many tenant farmers. However, when the campaign faltered due to funding difficulties after the split, tenants on the estates where landlords had successfully resisted, such as the Ponsonby estate in Youghal, or the Smith-Barry estate in Tipperary, were left to fend for themselves. Other evicted tenants were victims of earlier phases of land agitation. They were known as the 'wounded soldiers of the land war'. The bill included the recommendations of the Evicted Tenants' Commission, which had made its report earlier in the year, but also introduced the element of compulsion, with which the chief secretary, John Morley, could not agree. In his speech, McHugh stressed the advantageous terms being offered to landlords who wanted to sell their land, and he calculated the cost of evictions to the exchequer. He defended the plan of campaign and concluded by emphasising the urgency with which the Irish Party regarded the restitution of the evicted tenants, and in a dramatic flourish declared that he would 'rather abandon the hope of ever again beholding the shores of Ireland than abandon the hope of helping to secure for the evicted tenantry their reinstatement in their ancient homes'.[92] Despite McHugh's eloquence, the bill got no further than the second reading, and the problem of the evicted was not solved until 1907.

During the next session, McHugh concentrated on raising the issue of appointing magistrates, which led to a religious imbalance on the bench, with only a tiny proportion of Roman Catholics receiving commissions of the peace. Magistrates were appointed by the lord chancellor on the recommendation of the county lord lieutenants, who tended to select men from their own class and creed. McHugh raised the issue ten times during the session, constantly highlighting the disproportionate number of magistrates in Leitrim who were of the Protestant faith, although Roman Catholics constituted a huge majority in the county.[93] Morley was attempting to address the issue by sending recommendations directly to the lord chancellor, without the intervention of the county lieutenants. He achieved some success and gradually the number of Catholic magistrates increased.

McHugh raised this and other issues at question time, when a period of time was allocated for Irish business. It was usually attended by the chief secretary for Ireland. For most of his parliamentary career, McHugh contented himself with asking questions on a variety of subjects, most of which dealt with purely local matters. Some of the inquiries – such as the discontinuance of one of three daily mail trains from Drumshanbo to Ballinamore – seem incredibly trivial matters to be raised in parliament, but they were obviously of concern to his constituents.[94] Although his questions covered a wide range of topics, he concentrated on education, the position of tenant farmers, and the administration of justice. He did not become one of the orators of the party, and did not contribute to debates on major issues, such as home rule.

Although Gladstone succeeded in his second attempt to pass a home rule bill through the house of commons, it was rejected by the house of lords. He subsequently resigned and his successor, Lord Rosebery, did not inspire confidence in the Irish members. His government resigned in 1895, leading to a general election and a resounding victory for the Tories, who were to remain in power until 1906.

McHugh was returned unopposed for Leitrim North in the 1895 general election, and accepted a nomination to contest Clare East against William Redmond, brother of the leader of the anti-Parnellites. McHugh arrived in Clare just six days before polling day, and attempted a whirlwind tour of the constituency. The campaign was robust, with insults and allegations hurled by both sides. In Ennis, McHugh was faced with a hostile crowd and had to be escorted to his hotel by mounted policemen.[95] Despite the help of William O'Brien, McHugh was defeated by fifty-seven votes.[96] After the result was declared, he blamed his defeat on his late arrival in the constituency, and the 'gross falsehood' circulated about him, that he had been a member of a jury in Sligo which had convicted political prisoners from Clare.[97]

The election in Sligo North had been contested by Henry Harrison, a Parnellite who opposed Bernard Collery. The list of his proposers and assentors included members of the old National League, such as Thomas Connolly, Thady Kilgannon and James Fitzgerald, a solicitor who had refused to contribute to McHugh's testimonial fund in 1889.[98] In the aftermath of the 'Omagh scandal', caused by Healy's allegations that the party was handing over four seats in Ulster to the Liberals for money, McHugh stood firmly with McCarthy and Dillon in opposition to Healy. He was elected mayor of Sligo for the second time in 1895 and was re-elected to the post for the next three years. The defeat of the home rule bill, and the return to power of the Conservatives with a large majority, consigned the Irish Party to the political backbenches. The internal bickering in the party further damaged morale, and the contrast with Parnell's superbly disciplined party could not have been greater. During this period McHugh concentrated on local concerns. Although in editorials and in his public speeches he remained confident and optimistic, the unity that he urged among Irish nationalists seemed to be remote and elusive.

# Trials, Opportunities and Challenges

In January 1896, McHugh wrote to the Dublin newspapers suggesting that the forthcoming 'Convention of the Irish Race' should be used to work towards the reunion of Irish nationalists. McHugh's letter stressed the lack of major obstacles to unity; there was now no 'moral question', and no alliance with any other party in the house of commons; both parties had the same policies on the important Irish issues: home rule, land reform, evicted tenants and a Catholic university.[1] The grandiose sounding convention, planned since 1895, did not actually take place until September 1896, and it was a failure, as only the anti-Parnellites – minus the Healyites – attended. The following year McHugh was a member of a committee appointed by the Irish National Federation to meet with the representatives of the Irish National League to discuss the problem of the evicted tenants, but this attempt at combined action also failed.

In February 1896 John Dillon succeeded McCarthy as chairman of the anti-Parnellite party. Despite his best efforts, the party remained in disarray, and in January 1897, Healy, still a member of the party, founded a new organisation called the 'People's Rights Organisation', which advocated the independence of the constituencies in selecting their members, an idea which directly opposed Dillon's view that only a tightly disciplined party could achieve success. In such an atmosphere, it was not surprising that politics lost much of its prestige, and that the Federation was declining. Although fifteen Sligo branches were represented at the convention, most of them seemed to be inactive, as they did not send branch reports to the *Sligo Champion*. Outside of politics in rural areas, the co-operative movement, founded by Horace Plunkett in 1894, was becoming well-established. Bad weather again threatened to destroy the potato crop in the west.

During 1897, preparations were made by various groups to celebrate the centenary of the 1798 rebellion. The old fenian John O'Leary led one such group in Dublin. In November a meeting chaired by McHugh established the Sligo '98 club. The list of those in attendance included members of the Federation and those known to be 'Redmondites'.[2] By December, Ballymote and Gurteen had also founded '98 clubs. A police report asserted that the Ballymote club was controlled by the Irish Republican Brotherhood, but concluded that none of the clubs were 'active'.[3] In McHugh's first editorial of 1898, he expressed the hope that the celebrations would give 'new spirit' to the nationalists, and that 'combined action' would lead towards unity.[4] The first event in the celebrations took place in January, when a demonstration was held at Carricknagat, near Collooney, the site of a battle won by the French and Irish forces in 1798. 'Honest' John Dillon was present, and the crowd was so large that it was compared to the halycon days of the Land League. The resolutions passed at the meeting dealt with the unity of nationalists, the present 'distress' in the west, and the overtaxation of Ireland, which was the subject of a nationwide agitation.[5]

A long-standing demand of nationalists was the provision of a state-aided university for Roman Catholics. McHugh became involved in a committee of lay people in Sligo, which held several meetings to discuss the issue. The dire situation facing many of his constituents also claimed his attention when

PATRICK A. MCHUGH ELOQUENT.

3. McHugh as orator, as seen by the *St James's Gazette*, February 1898.

evictions began on the former Tottenham estate. McHugh, along with a priest and a doctor, accompanied the bailiffs around Kiltyclogher, followed by a crowd of several hundred people. The descriptions of the squalid cabins in which the people lived, are reminiscent of the Famine era. In one such dwelling the occupants were lying on bundles of straw: 'This cabin presented one of the most fearful pictures of desolation and poverty that the eye of man could look upon'.[6] Despite the various measures introduced to improve the conditions of tenant farmers, in areas such as Leitrim, where agricultural holdings were small and unproductive, farmers were not benefitting and lived at the mercy of weather conditions.

The condition of the west of Ireland was raised by McHugh in the parliamentary session of 1898. He described the scenes at Kiltyclogher, and explained the reluctance of his countrymen to go to the workhouse to seek relief. He condemned the under-funding of the Congested Districts Board, 'the only board in which we in Ireland have any confidence'.[7] He was called to order several times by the Speaker for not speaking to the amendment, and his performance in the house was noted in the English press.

The only hope offered to the Irish at Westminster was the promise of a new system of local government. Nationalist leaders such as Dillon and Davitt viewed the bill with some suspicion, but McHugh welcomed the bill when it was introduced, describing it as a'revolutionary measure', which would ensure that Col Cooper 'will have just as much influence and voice in the management of the county as Paddy Clancy the sweep'.[8] The local government bill was part of the government's policy of 'constructive unionism', which was seen as 'killing home rule with kindness'. Local government was to be administered by county, rural and urban district councils, which were to be elected triennially by a parliamentary electorate, and by women ratepayers, who could also stand for election for the rural and urban district councils. These councils assumed responsibility for roads, public works, public health and the housing of labourers. Rural district councillors were also to serve as poor law guardians, and they were to assume control of poor relief, dispensaries and workhouse hospitals. County councils were to maintain major roads, prisons, courthouses and hospitals. All local charges were to be made into a single rate, which was to be collected by the county council, and it controlled the funds of the rural district councils. Boroughs were to be urban district councils, and were to be elected by a much larger electorate. The urban district could levy its own rates. The grand jury only maintained its judicial function. The first elections for the new councils were to be held in March 1899.[9]

McHugh contributed to the bill when it reached the committee stage, and on the question of compensating the barony cess collectors for the loss of their posts, he caused uproar when he suggested that most of them had achieved their positions due to being 'the illegitimate sons of the grand jurors'.[10] When the bill became law at the end of July, he explained its provisions to his readers, regretting the 'intolerant, unjust and indefensible provision which excludes clergymen from the Councils', which he saw as being directed at Roman Catholic priests.[11]

While the bill was going through parliament, the movement to commemorate the anniversary of the 1798 rising grew in strength, and in Sligo a ladies' committee was formed. Many of those involved in the new clubs, such as John McLoughlin, were also prominent in the local Federation branch, and he was also treasurer of the co-operative society. The '98 clubs usually took the names of patriots associated with the rebellion, such as Wolfe Tone (Tubbercurry), Teeling (Gurteen), and Robert Emmet (Ballymote). The Gurteen club organised a meeting which was addressed by Maud Gonne, and the Cloonacool club held celebrations to mark the anniversary of Emmet's birthday. A convention of clubs was held in Sligo, which decided not to affiliate with either of the two Dublin executives, and urged the two groups to amalgamate. A resolution was passed that a suitable memorial be erected at Carricknagat.[12] A further convention approved of the union of the two national executives, and decided to erect a second memorial in Sligo town.[13]

The '98 celebrations led to a proposal by five members of the corporation to re-name several of the town's streets in honour of patriots such as Grattan, Tone and O'Connell. As the proposal included naming one of the streets after Parnell, it caused some acrimony, and it was defeated.[14] McHugh was not in favour of honouring Parnell while nationalists were divided. The foundation stone of the memorial at Carricknagat – which was to be a statue of Bartholomew Teeling, the hero of the battle – was unveiled amidst much ceremony in September. It was planned that Dillon, Davitt, Healy and two Parnellite MPs, Clancy and Field, would attend, but they all sent their apologies. They were not yet willing to share the same platform, and instead, the crowd heard from McHugh, Collery and Joseph Devlin from Belfast.[15]

By the end of the summer of 1898, public attention was drawn to the emergence of a new organisation, the United Irish League, which had been founded in Mayo in January by William O'Brien, who had been living in Westport since his resignation from parliamentary politics in 1895. He witnessed the poverty of tenants who tried to scrape a living from small, uneconomic holdings, which were contiguous to large grazing farms. The Congested Districts Board, which had been established in 1891 to improve conditions in areas such as Mayo, was seriously underfunded, and unable to function efficiently. O'Brien came to the conclusion that the only solution to congestion was the redistribution of the large grazing farms, also known as 'untenanted' land. The high prices for beef and cattle, and the low labour costs involved, made grazing a profitable investment. Grazing lands were often held on an 'eleven month' system, where the owner let the land for eleven months, thereby avoiding any responsibilities under the land acts. The grazing issue had been raised by the Land League, but had not been pursued to any extent.

O'Brien, despairing of the parliamentarians, hoped that the new organisation would also bring about unity in the nationalist ranks.

The first meeting of the United Irish League – the name was chosen as a deliberate reference to the '98 centenary – was held in Westport in January 1898. The speakers included John Dillon and the Parnellite MP Tim Harrington. The new organisation was confined to west Mayo for the first few months of its existence. Large graziers were visited by deputations of members, and asked to hand over their land. The traditional methods of agrarian agitation were used, such as boycotting, threatening letters, and preventing small farmers from sending their cattle to graze on the large farms. The graziers were treated as 'land grabbers', with whom they were compared, as much of their land included the former farms of evicted tenants. Although he had some help from local activists like John O'Donnell and John MacHale, much of the burden of organisation and finance was left to O'Brien. Of his former colleagues, only Michael Davitt assisted him in his work.[16]

In Sligo, the activities of the United Irish League were known and admired by people in the summer of 1898. The weakness of the Federation was highlighted in a branch report from Keash, which threatened that if no remedial action was taken against poverty in the parish, 'we must only seek the protection of the "West Mayo League", which we regard as the coming great movement'.[17] This confidence in the United Irish League was also expressed at a '98 convention, which was specifically convened to discuss the new League. McHugh presided over the meeting, and in his speech he asserted that the only solution to the cycle of poverty and distress in the west was the compulsory sale of land which was given over to 'sheep and bullocks'. In his opinion, the primary importance of the new League was its object of unifying nationalists, who could forget the 'wretched wrangles of the past seven years'.[18] When a Ballymote delegate asked how such an organisation could prosper given the disunity of the nationalist leaders, McHugh replied that popular pressure could compel the MPs to work together, which was how William O'Brien saw the role of the League. A resolution was passed by the convention which compared the United Irish League to the Land League, and expressed support for its aims and principles.

The first two branches to be established in the county were at Sooey and Conway's Cross, two small villages in south Sligo. In Sooey, the committees of the Irish National Federation and the '98 club became the committee of the new branch. McHugh and John O'Dowd, now chairman of the Tubbercurry board of guardians, attended the launching of the movement in Conway's Cross. McHugh, again comparing the United Irish League to the Land League, announced that one of the major duties of the new branches would be to ensure that 'proper candidates' were selected for the forthcoming council elections.[19] McHugh saw the United Irish League as being different in character from the National League and the National Federation; it was not to be subordinate to the political parties, and it was a genuine grass roots organisation. In September, he accompanied O'Brien to Labasheeda in County Clare to address a meeting, and was physically assaulted by a 'grabber' he had publicly named.[20] He also spoke at a large meeting in Elphin, County Roscommon, a Parnellite stronghold, and Ballycastle in Mayo, where he denied that the policy of redistributing land was 'socialistic'.[21]

O'Brien came to Sligo for the unveiling of the foundation stone of the '98 memorial, and in his speech praised McHugh , who was 'doing a hundred men's part'.[22] In his diary O'Brien also paid tribute to McHugh's efforts, describing him as 'the one man from whom I can expect help', and on his visit to Sligo, observing him on his home territory, he commented that his 'popularity exceeds by long odds that of any other members of the party'.[23] He also found that McHugh could be unreliable at times, and made several veiled references in his diary to what he saw as McHugh's problems with alcohol.

A police report compiled in October 1898, stated that there were twenty-seven branches of the United Irish League in Mayo, but only two in Sligo, and they were seen as 'practically inoperative'.[24] During October and November however, several branches were formed. An editorial in the *Sligo Champion* of 22 October announced the establishment of the Sligo borough branch after a meeting in the town. The main purpose of the League was declared to be the finding of a permanent solution to the problem of recurring famines in the west of Ireland. The break-up of the grazing lands was seen as vital to the solution of the problem, although it was admitted that large-scale grazing was not widespread in Sligo and Leitrim. People not engaged in agriculture could, through the League, agitate against the overtaxation of Ireland, campaign for a Catholic university, and organise for the local government elections. There was as yet no formal constitution, and the only rule was that 'all controversial subjects as between Irish Nationalists shall be excluded from discussion at meetings of the league', and a resolution was adopted which echoed the principles of the United Irishmen: 'this club is constituted for the purpose of forwarding a brotherhood of affection, a commission of rights, and a union of power among Irishmen'.[25] Throughout the following months branches of the United Irish League were established in Bunnanadden, Grange, Dromore West, Cliffoney and Ballisodare. Many of the inaugural meetings took the form of a public demonstration, usually addressed by McHugh and O'Dowd.

The municipal elections were held under the provisions of the local government act, which increased the number of those eligible to vote from 366 to 1,888.[26] The elections were a success for the United Irish League, and four 'Labour' candidates were also elected. The first few months of 1899 were dominated by preparations for the forthcoming elections to the new councils. Arrangements were made to hold conventions organised on a parliamentary constituency basis. The Sligo South convention was held in Ballymote, but the sub-sheriff, Col Coffey, had refused to allow the courthouse to be used by the

United Irish League. In a celebrated incident, McHugh sent for a sledge-hammer and proceeded to break down the door. He then led the cheering delegates into the courthouse, and presided over the meeting. The convention selected candidates for the county council election, and out of nine electoral divisions, there were only three contests. Those who secured nomination included League activists such as John O'Dowd, and the veteran Nicholas Devine.[27]

A police report claimed that the convention had been called by McHugh and O'Dowd, and that it had been opposed by the Roman Catholic clergy, who wished to ensure that men 'of some education and means' were chosen as county councillors. McHugh was seen as favouring 'advanced Nationalists', and was accused of having overturned the selection of the Riverstown branch, and choosing Charles McSteen, a farmer, instead of a local shopkeeper who had the approval of the priests of the parish. Divisions were also reported from Sligo town, between McHugh and the Trades Council, because he withdrew his support for its candidates, due to opposition from the clergy, and 'other leading men of the town'.[28] A later report suggested that there was 'considerable friction between McHugh and the clergy, because of his support for the 'extremists' in the county.[29] The clergy may have disapproved of the League's principles, which favoured the small farmers against the large graziers, many of whom were prominent businessmen and merchants. William O'Brien had also faced clerical opposition in Mayo during the first year of the League's existence.

McHugh attended the Connaught convention of the League, which was held in Claremorris on 30 January. A constitution was drawn up which placed home rule as the first objective of the League, instead of the agrarian aims previously enunciated. Along with the compulsory sale of grazing lands and the 'abolition of landlordism', the traditional demands were made for the reinstatement of the evicted tenants, a Catholic university, labourers' dwellings, and the fostering of Irish manufacturing. A new element was the support for the preservation of the Irish language. The convention also provided for the establishment of a provincial directory which would be responsible for the general policy of the League, and for the arbitration of disputes.[30]

The local elections aroused considerable interest among the public, who for the first time could participate in the running of the county. The number of those seeking election was applauded by McHugh, who saw the interest in the elections as proof of the 'latent political energy' of the Irish people. He hoped for 'friendly rivalry' among the nationalist candidates, and promised to report impartially on their campaigns.[31] Each local branch was given the freedom to select their own candidates for the district councils. Every electoral division elected two councillors from very small areas. A meeting in Keash, chaired by the local parish priest, selected candidates for several divisions, and as the division of Drumrat was divided between the parishes of Keash and Ballymote, it was left to the Culfadda branch to decide whether to confer with the Ballymote branch.[32] Several disputes arose within branches, and some candidates were asked to withdraw. If a branch selected a candidate who did not find favour with a neighbouring branch, allegations were made that the man was a landlord, or that he was 'anti-nationalist'.

The county council elections however, caused the greatest amount of friction, as the post of county councillor was obviously seen as more prestigious than that of district councillor. The dispute in Riverstown between John Judge, and McHugh's favoured candidate Charles McSteen, even led to the establishment of a rival branch of the United Irish League, which called itself the 'People's' branch, a title which had a Healyite ring. Another dispute arose over the representation of the Kilmacowen division. McHugh was berated by the Collooney branch for declaring his support for John McLoughlin of the Sooey branch, despite his promise to remain impartial.[33] McHugh defended himself by pointing to McLoughlin's past record in the nationalist cause, and described him as 'a recognised captain in leading and organising the Nationalist forces of Co. Sligo against landlordism and ascendancy'.[34] Once again, McHugh found himself on the opposite side to the clergy. McLoughlin's opponent Edward Mulrooney, had the support of Fr. Brennan, a local priest. He continued to campaign for John McLoughlin, but was careful not to criticise Mulrooney.

The elections returned many League activists to the new councils. McSteen and McLoughlin were both successful, although in other areas candidates who had received McHugh's approval were defeated. In the Kilmactranny division, Captain McTernan, described by the *Champion* as a 'castle hack', was elected, while Col Howley, a landlord who was favoured by both McHugh and the clergy, was defeated. The new councillors included O'Dowd and Nicholas Devine. Some county councillors were also elected to the district councils. McHugh was elected as a representative from the borough to the county council, topping the poll with over 1,000 votes.[35] Despite their alleged animosity towards McHugh, the Sligo Trades Council called on his fellow councillors to elect him as chairman of the new council and, at its first meeting, he was elected unanimously.[36]

By virtue of being chairman of the county council, McHugh was once again a magistrate at petty sessions courts. He also became chairman of the board of governors of the lunatic asylum, and the governor of the infirmary. He was still a town councillor and attended meetings of the corporation. He continued to preside over meetings of the Sligo branch and of the north Sligo executive of the United Irish League, and attended meetings of the provincial directory. He was involved in the political life of the county at various levels, while still representing his native county at Westminster. While home rule still remained the ultimate goal of Irish nationalist politicians, it seemed unattainable for the time being, so McHugh devoted his energies to politics at a local level. His resignation from the county council after just three months therefore comes as a surprise, and in public he gave his reason as being 'of a purely private and personal nature'.[37] His fellow councillors however, did not appear to be very shocked, and some rivalry developed as to who would succeed to the chair. McHugh condemned Collery for canvassing for the post, as he felt that the vice-chairman, John O'Dowd, should be proposed automatically. O'Dowd was unopposed as chairman, a position he was to hold for twenty years.

This temporary setback did not stop McHugh's activities, and his work for the United Irish League actually increased at this time. The newspaper was successful, and he moved to larger premises in Wine Street, and for a few months, two issues were published weekly. When a meeting due to be held in Dromahair, County Leitrim was proclaimed by a Resident Magistrate, McHugh saw this as an attempt to 'deprive my constituents and myself of our constitutional rights of Public Meeting and Free Speech'.[38] He also saw the ban as a challenge, and he was determined to speak at Dromahair. The meeting was organised in support of four men, two of whom were councillors, who were charged with interfering with a receiver in the course of his duties. McHugh travelled from Sligo and was joined by Haviland Burke, a Dublin Parnellite, and they managed to evade the police and spoke at different times to the vast crowds assembled in the town.

The outbreak of the Boer war in October 1899 provided a focus for Irish nationalist opposition to the Westminster regime. Public bodies such as Sligo County Council passed a resolution of sympathy with the Boers, and also decided to follow the example of other county councils and fly a green flag from the courthouse, where they met in the old grand jury room. The adoption of the pro-Boer resolution led to John O'Dowd's removal from the magistracy by the lord chancellor. When the county council attempted to raise the green flag, it was taken down by the police, but the councillors did succeed in flying another one from the town hall.[39] Similar events took place throughout the country, as councils attempted to assert their new-found authority.

The year had seen a rapid growth in the United Irish League. In Sligo, the number of branches rose from twenty-four on 1 February 1899, to thirty-six at the end of November, and in Leitrim, where the League had a slow beginning, the number of branches increased from seven to thirty-one during the same period.[40] The rapid growth in Leitrim was partly due to McHugh's extensive campaigning in the county. The League was supported by many MPs from both sides of the Irish nationalist divide, but was looked upon with some suspicion by the leading members of the parties, who were nervously aware of an impending general election. John Dillon had resigned as chairman of the anti-Parnellites in February 1899, and the position was deliberately left vacant until complicated negotiations resulted in the reunion of the Irish party, which public opinion and the dramatic growth of the United Irish League demanded. On the latter point, F.S.L. Lyons observed that 'if the politicians were not to be submerged in the swiftly flowing tide then they must bestir themselves'.[41]

After nearly one year of fitful talks, the party was reunited at the end of January 1900. It had been decided a few months earlier that a Parnellite would be chairman, and at the eleventh hour, John Redmond was elected. Dillon was not in favour of Redmond, but when urged by William O'Brien, he supported him for the leadership of the party. O'Brien believed that Redmond, rather than Harrington, would be more open to persuasion regarding O'Brien's view of the supremacy of the United Irish League. McHugh, who had been virulent in his condemnation of Redmond during the years of the split, spoke against his nomination, but Redmond was elected unanimously.[42] Although McHugh had championed the reunion of the party, he now purported to be indifferent, and dismissed the event as 'a tardy recognition of certain truths', and he claimed that the event had been brought about by the League: 'the people of Ireland are the masters of their Parliamentary representatives'.[43]

The League showed its authority in the political arena by selecting John O'Dowd to contest the Sligo North by-election caused by the resignation of Bernard Collery. McHugh spoke at a meeting in support of another League candidate and organiser, John O'Donnell, who was chosen to replace Michael Davitt, who had resigned his seat in protest against the Boer war. McHugh attacked the 'Dissentionists', who nominated Major John MacBride, who was leading the Irish Brigade fighting for the Boers. MacBride's supporters included Arthur Griffith and Maud Gonne, and McHugh seemed to believe that Healy was behind them.[44] Both United Irish League candidates were elected, and the reunited parliamentary party had had no say in their selection.

In June 1900 the United Irish League was deemed to be the official organisation of the nationalist party, and Redmond was elected as its national president. The convention consisted of delegates from branches, divisional executives, county, borough and district councils, and labour associations. A constitution was drawn up for the League: each branch was to send six delegates to a divisional executive, which was to be formed in each parliamentary constituency. The executive was to arbitrate on complaints from local branches, and retained half of the monies collected locally by branches, who were to keep one quarter, while the remaining quarter went to the national directory, which was to be the central body; each division sent one representative to a provincial directory.[45]

When a general election was announced in September, a series of resolutions was passed by the national directory of the League, which governed the selection of parliamentary candidates. Conventions were to be summoned by the divisional executive in each constituency, and were to be chaired by the president of the executive, not an outsider. Delegates were to be drawn from local branches, the clergy, trade and labour associations, nationalist councillors, and members of such groups as the GAA, the Irish National Foresters and the Ancient Order of Hibernians. Candidates were expected to be staunch supporters of the League.[46] The United Irish League therefore, was, in theory, to control and direct elections with very little interference from the parliamentary party. As has been seen, prior to the split, the party organisation, and especially the conventions had been completely under the control of Parnell and his 'lieutenants'. The legacy of the years of disunity had led to a distrust of the parliamentarians, and the system of centralised control over the movement. As time went by however, the national directory came to be dominated by MPs, despite William O'Brien's determination to avoid this situation.[47]

In the general election, McHugh was opposed by Charles Singleton, the Unionist candidate, who was based in London. This was to be the last time McHugh was faced with a contested election. He had a convincing win over Singleton, but 40 per cent of the electorate abstained from voting, probably because the result was a foregone conclusion.[48] John O'Dowd, the sitting MP for the northern division, chose to sit for his native Sligo South. Thomas Curran, who had been the member of the southern division since 1892, had incurred the wrath of the League because of his lengthy absence from his constituency, and he was deemed to be not only a 'place hunter', but also a 'Healyite'. The vacancy in north Sligo was filled by William McKillop, a Glasgow merchant, who was recommended by John Dillon and William O'Brien. This 'parachuting' of a candidate who had no connection whatsoever with the constituency, seems strange, considering the emphasis placed on local organisations. Indeed, at the convention there were objections raised to his nomination, but the *Champion* dismissed these 'malcontents'.[49] Several United Irish League activists, such as Conor O'Kelly, the first chairman of Mayo County Council, and Haviland Burke were elected. None of them was to assume positions of leadership in the party, which remained dominated by the generation that served with Parnell.[50]

McHugh was now facing a sterner challenge in the form of a criminal prosecution. He had avoided a charge of criminal libel which was instituted when he called the Resident Magistrate in Dromahair a 'hired Removable'. However, he faced other charges arising from a series of articles he wrote about 'jury packing' in Sligo. The offending articles were written during the trial of two League organisers from Mayo. Arthur Muffeny and Anthony Maguire were charged with conspiracy against a local 'grabber'. They received six months imprisonment with hard labour at the winter assizes in Sligo. McHugh attacked the selection of the jury, during which twenty-two Roman Catholic jurors were challenged by the crown, leading to an exclusively Protestant jury. He saw this as a 'violation of law and justice', as they differed in politics and religion from the 'traversers'.[51] On three occasions he even published the names of the jurors, and listed their addresses and occupations.[52]

McHugh was charged with 'vilifying' the judge and the jurors, but at the trial a Dublin jury could not agree on a verdict.[53] At a subsequent trial however, he was found guilty on a charge of seditious libel. The indictment described McHugh as an 'evil disposed person', who had 'wickedly and maliciously contriving and intending to bring the administration of justice in this kingdom into contempt and to scandalise and vilify jurors'.[54] The lord chief justice defined seditious libel as the intention to bring the administration of justice into 'contempt and disgrace', and publishing matter which would accomplish this intention; he admonished McHugh for suggesting that the jurors had perjured themselves, and for publishing their names.[55] McHugh received a sentence of six months imprisonment in Kilmainham jail, without hard labour, and he was to be treated as a 'misdemeanant of the first division', which allowed him to wear his own clothes, to have relaxed visiting hours, and a large cell apart from other prisoners.[56] The charge of seditious libel was so unusual that it was widely commented upon.

While he was imprisoned, the work of the United Irish League continued, and attracted the attention of the police. The county was considered to be 'disturbed' by the authorities, especially the districts of Ballymote and Tubbercurry, where graziers and 'grabbers' were boycotted.[57] Special instructions were issued regarding League activities in these areas, and the police were urged to be vigilant in their surveillance. The press was seen to be essential to the League, and the chief secretary, George Wyndham, suggested that prosecutions against the press should be carefully selected, and proposed that McHugh could be threatened with the loss of his privileges in prison if his paper continued to publish boycotting resolutions from branches.[58] The *Sligo Champion* was described as 'a leading source of mischief in Sligo and surrounding Counties. Where it circulates the people live in dread of having their names published as guilty of offences against the League'.[59] Out of a list of thirteen newspapers which published 'intimidatory' notices, the *Sligo Champion*, the *Irish People* and the *Waterford Star* were singled out as being the worst offenders.[60]

McHugh was released from prison in October, and was met by Tim Harrington MP, lord mayor of Dublin, and John O'Dowd. He was entertained by several city councillors, and then took the train back to Sligo where he was welcomed by cheering crowds. At a special meeting of Dublin Corporation a proposal was passed to confer the freedom of the city on McHugh, citing:

> the many and eminent services rendered to the cause of Irish Nationality . . . and more particularly to give practical expression of our appreciation of his spirited protest against the infamous system of Jury Packing under which British Law is administered in Ireland.[61]

By early November he was in New York, accompanying John Redmond and Thomas O'Donnell MP on a fund-raising tour during which they travelled to Boston, Chicago and Washington, where they met President Theodore Roosevelt at the White House. McHugh and Redmond were now on very cordial terms, and had corresponded during his incarceration in Kilmainham.[62]

The use of coercion against the United Irish League seemed to lead to an increase in its activities. At the spring assizes the judge told the grand jury that the 'law is superseded, and a reign of terror exists in several districts'.[63] The League operated like the Land League; branches denounced those who broke its rules, and anyone associating with such 'obnoxious' people was similarly condemned, unless they appeared before the branch and apologised for their 'transgression'. From time to time several branches met together in a 'conference' to discuss issues of mutual concern. The north Sligo executive discussed the forthcoming local elections, and decided that all councillors should take a pledge promising to give preference to tenders to United Irish League members.[64] The members thus saw themselves as separate from non-members, and gave out rewards and punishments as appropriate. Philip Bull claims that the League saw itself as an 'alternative' or *de facto* government, and that its function became 'the statement of a wider social unity, a means of defining a community identity, an expression of a sense of distinctiveness'.[65]

In April McHugh and Redmond were both presented with the freedom of Dublin city, and in his speech he joked that he was being honoured because he had broken the law.[66] Ironically, his freedom was to be severely curtailed in the following months, as writs arrived from all quarters. In February, he was sued for libel by W.R. Fenton, the solicitor to the county council. He also served as crown prosecutor for Sligo, and McHugh had objected to retaining his services while he was prosecuting members of the League. At a subsequent meeting of the county council, it was decided to dispense with his services, and Fenton claimed that McHugh had conspired to induce the council to sack him. A Belfast jury awarded Fenton the enormous sum of £3,500 despite the efforts of Tim Healy, McHugh's barrister.[67] McHugh was adjudged to be a bankrupt, and court officials took possession of his home and office. This was a serious blow, because it meant that he was forbidden to sit in the house of commons, and was only entitled to retain his seat for twelve months. His manager, Bernard McTernan, published the newspaper for several months under the new title the *Sligo Nationalist*.

While McHugh was awaiting the outcome of the libel proceedings, he received a summons for contempt, because he had published a boycotting notice of the Highwood branch regarding an estate which was being administered by the Land Judges' Court.[68] Another summons was served on him in May, charging him with taking part in a criminal conspiracy 'to compel Charles Anderson not to occupy a farm at Springfield'.[69] He was arrested in Dublin and put on a train to Sligo, where he was brought before the petty sessions court. For calling the magistrates 'damned liars', he was found guilty of contempt, and imprisoned.[70] He received a sentence of three months, and was released in September, when he made a statement to the press regarding his status as a bankrupt. He claimed to be indifferent as to whether he would enter the house of commons again.[71] A select committee of the house of commons was appointed to enquire into the proceedings of the court case, and McHugh was allowed to appear before it to give evidence.

On the original charge of conspiracy, he conducted his own defence. He refused to be bound to not publishing boycotting resolutions, and a two month jail sentence was handed down. The only good news for McHugh was that the *Champion* had been bought by his friends and placed in his wife's name. On his release, he went abroad to recover his health and, despite his bankruptcy, he travelled to Egypt and Palestine for several months. He missed the passage through parliament of the Wyndham Land Act, which although it did not include compulsory purchase, enabled large scale purchase by tenants, and was finally to create the peasant proprietorship which had been a nationalist demand for over twenty years.[72]

McHugh returned to Sligo, and as he set out for Longford to meet Bourke Cockran, the distinguished Sligo-born US statesman, he was arrested on the original contempt charge. Although in theory the sentence was unlimited, he was released after only two weeks. The by-election in Leitrim North caused by his bankruptcy was fixed for October 1903, and at a convention in Drumkeeran, McHugh's elderly father Peter, was selected to fill the vacancy.[73] The high sheriff however, received nomination papers from both McHughs. There had been rumours that a Unionist candidate would contest the vacancy, but when this did not materialise, Peter McHugh's papers were withdrawn, and P.A. was declared elected.[74] This strategy had been decided at the convention. The return of an undischarged bankrupt was forbidden by statute in England, but constitutional experts could not find a similar provision for Ireland.

The Wyndham Land Act was the main topic of discussion among nationalists during this period. The *Sligo Champion* called it 'the greatest measure ever passed by the British parliament for the improvement of the agrarian situation in Ireland', but qualified this praise by stating that the act was not a 'final settlement' of the land question.[75] However, influential leaders such as Dillon and Davitt began to criticise the act in public. Dillon spoke to his constituents in Swinford, and condemned the act as being too beneficial to the landlords, and attacked the policy of 'conciliation' with Unionists which William O'Brien was pursuing. The main nationalist daily the *Freeman's Journal*, edited by Thomas Sexton, was also hostile to the land act, and faced with such opposition, O'Brien resigned from the party in November. McHugh lamented his decision and paid tribute to O'Brien's 'inspiring enthusiasm and transcendant genius, his chivalry and self-sacrifice, his dauntless courage and matchless eloquence'.[76] He could not, despite his admiration for O'Brien, agree with his new concept of political relationships in Ireland. He found himself unable to contemplate such a radical change in his political viewpoint, which automatically consigned landlords and unionists to the position of the enemy.[77]

By January 1904 he was critical of the portions of the act dealing with 'untenanted' lands, and the problem of congestion, and at a meeting of the national directory of the United Irish League, he proposed a resolution which described the act as 'utterly worthless so far as the relief of congestion in the

West of Ireland is concerned'.[78] At the opening of parliament he proposed an amendment to the Address to the King, in which he explained the problems of congestion in the west, especially in Mayo, and he reminded the government that the alternative to conciliation was 'continued conflict'.[79] Some tenants faced obdurate landlords, who either wanted too high a purchase price, or were not interested in selling. The Culfadda branch of the League met to consider an offer by an owner of a grazing farm, and complained about the lack of success in breaking up the 'ranches', and in Achonry, the members actually opposed the League's policy, when they demonstrated against the Congested Districts Board's plan to settle tenants from Mayo in the area.[80]

The general election of 1906 returned the Liberals to power with a large majority. McHugh was nominated and returned for the seats of Sligo North and Leitrim North. At the Sligo convention he declined to state which constituency he would represent, but he ultimately chose the Sligo seat. His successor in Leitrim North was Charles Dolan, whose father had been a political activist. The size of the Liberal majority meant that the Irish party was not crucial to the government's survival, but they remained optimistic about an imminent home rule bill.

A Royal Commission was established in 1906 to inquire into congestion in Ireland. It was known as the Dudley Commission, and in the spring of 1907, it visited Sligo and Leitrim to gather evidence. Witnesses were proposed by League branches, county and district councils, landlords and the local bishop. When the members of the Commission met at Tubbercurry, John McLoughlin, who was nominated by the county council as a witness, informed them that over 50 per cent of agricultural holdings were under fifteen acres. In some areas, the Congested Districts Board was powerless if the land was not congested. Several witnesses referred to the importance of money sent from the USA and England, and a Tubbercurry shopkeeper estimated that at Christmas, he cashed money orders to the value of £800. In Manorhamilton, 73 per cent of the holdings had a valuation of less than £10, and seasonal migration to Scotland was very common.[81]

In 1907, Irish nationalists were eagerly awaiting the announcement of a home rule bill by the government. In May however, when the chief secretary, Augustine Birrell, introduced the Irish Council Bill in the house of commons, it was perceived as a hopelessly inadequate measure, and it was later withdrawn. The long-awaited bill caused great disappointment, and to some, it showed up the inadequacy of parliamentary agitation. Charles Dolan, McHugh's successor as the member for Leitrim North, proposed a resolution at the north Leitrim executive of the United Irish League, calling on the Parliamentary Party to withdraw from Westminster, as home rule did not seem to be any closer than it was in O'Connell's day. The resolution was passed, and at a meeting of the national directory, Dolan supported a similar motion proposed by Thomas O'Donnell, which only received three votes.[82] This abstentionist policy had been propounded by Arthur Griffith, who led a disparate group of small organisations, which in 1908 were to amalgamate under the title 'Sinn Féin'. Along with the secession of Irish MPs, Griffith also advocated economic self-sufficiency and the development of native industries.

McHugh, though critical of this 'new-fangled' policy, did not condemn Dolan too harshly, as he believed him to be under the influence of 'a handful of Dublin cranks', but he called on him to resign his seat.[83] Although Dolan announced his intention to resign, he delayed doing so for another six months, presumably to gain time to publicise his new beliefs. The first public meeting since his declaration in favour of the 'Sinn Féin policy', was held in Manorhamilton, and the speakers included McHugh and Dolan. The latter castigated Westminster as a 'farce', and allegedly described Isaac Butt as a 'Wind-Bag'.[84] Arthur Griffith's newspaper *Sinn Féin*, declared that McHugh's speech was a 'painful surprise to us all', and repeated accusations that Redmond had demanded a high price for land he had sold to his tenants.[85] The north Leitrim executive rescinded its resolution concerning abstention, and called on Dolan to resign.

McHugh defended the record of the Irish at Westminster and listed its achievements, all accomplished by constitutional agitation, and he claimed that the only difference between the party and Sinn Féin was the question of attendance at the house of commons.[86] Dolan continued to explain his policies in north Leitrim, and some League members supported him. A national fund was established by Griffith's National Council for his election campaign. Among those who spoke on his behalf was Sean MacDermott, a native of Kiltyclogher and a full-time organiser for Sinn Féin. In November, John Redmond arrived in Sligo to receive the freedom of the borough, and the occasion was used to celebrate his leadership and the achievements of the Irish party.[87] He also paid a visit to north Leitrim to address a meeting in Drumkeeran. McHugh missed both events due to illness. His health did not improve, and he was absent also from a home rule demonstration in Sligo, which was addressed by Joseph Devlin, John O'Dowd and Thomas Kettle. It was rumoured that he was either dead or dying, and he felt compelled to issue a statement explaining his condition from his hospital bed in Dublin.[88]

By the new year, he had recovered and he became involved in the by-election campaign. He condemned Dolan for fomenting division, especially at a time when William O'Brien and Tim Healy had rejoined the party. At the north Leitrim convention, the United Irish League selected Francis Meehan, a Manorhamilton businessman to contest the vacancy. He was described by McHugh as 'a man of substance and standing', who would have an easy victory, as only the ignorant, 'cranks' and unionists would vote for Dolan.[89] McHugh played a prominent role in the campaign, and spoke at several meetings. *Sinn Féin* reminded its readers that he had also directed the by-election against Parnell in 1891 and revealed that he had applied to join the

Liberal club in London.[90] The following week it gleefully announced that he had withdrawn his application. The campaign was eventful, and several times the supporters of both candidates engaged in running battles. Parnell's sister, Anna, came to Leitrim to speak on Dolan's behalf, and she received a rough reception from some of Meehan's supporters. Both sides were accused of importing 'hooligans' to intimidate their opponents. Meehan won the election with 3,103 votes to Dolan's 1,157, a very respectable result for Sinn Féin, considering they were opposed by the formidable resources of the parliamentary party.[91] Sinn Féin did not contest any more parliamentary seats until after the 1916 rising, and Dolan subsequently emigrated to the USA, although his brother James was elected in the Sinn Féin landslide in 1918.[92]

The anti-grazier agitation was reaching a climax during 1907 and 1908, but McHugh did not take part in the 'cattle-driving' movement, which involved removing cattle from the grazier's land at night to leave them wandering around the roads. This phase of the agrarian agitation was known as the 'ranch war', and it was led by MPs such as Laurence Ginnell and J.P. Farrell.[93] Although Sligo was not a ranching county, several cattle-drives took place, and in one such incident at Riverstown, a young man was shot dead by the police.[94] McHugh advised tenants to boycott the graziers rather than break the law.

A convention called early in 1909 to discuss the United Irish League's attitude to Birrell's proposed land bill, witnessed William O'Brien's final departure from the movement he had founded. He was shouted down by the audience when he attempted to propose the holding of a conference similar to one held in 1902, which formed the basis of the Wyndham Act.

In May, McHugh was still stressing the importance of local League branches being organised and ready to fight another election, and urging those eligible to apply for the new old age pension. Later that month however, he was taken ill and died in a Dublin hospital. The years of frenetic activity, of countless open-air meetings, often held in appalling conditions, and his time in prison had all taken their toll on his health. His funeral took place in Sligo, his adopted home. His political opponents in the town paid tribute to 'the champion of the masses', and 'the poor man's friend'.[95] McHugh's successor as the member for Sligo North was Thomas Scanlan, who held the seat until the 1918 election, when both Sligo seats were won by Sinn Féin. It is unlikely, despite the genuine popularity in which he was held, that McHugh's fate would have been any different, since the old Irish party, for which he had laboured for over twenty years, and to which he remained loyal through the years of dissension and sterility, was consigned by the 'cranks' of Sinn Féin 'into the limbo of forgotten things'.[96]

# Conclusion

This study has examined P.A. McHugh's life and career as a politician and newspaper editor. During his early career, he was involved with politics on a purely local level, through the Irish National League and Sligo corporation. He was not one of the 'eighty-six of eighty-six', led by Parnell, and imbued with his glamour and charisma. To them, the future looked bright and some form of legislative independence seemed to be a certainty. At this time, McHugh was an enthusiastic grass-roots supporter of the party, and he helped to organise the party machinery in Sligo, although as has been seen, ultimate control rested with a small group of men close to Parnell.

The Parnell split led to a breakdown in allegiances, and although McHugh did not initially condemn the 'Chief', when he did take a stance his language and tone were as bitter as any of his contemporaries. The split in the party gave him the opportunity to move to a broader stage, when he was elected to the Westminster parliament. Although he was a very well-known figure in the west of Ireland, he was to remain essentially a local politician, who did not rise to a position of prominence in the party, and like most of the Irish members, did not take any interest in issues which did not affect Ireland. His eager welcome for the new institutions of local government contrasted with the suspicious attitude of Michael Davitt and John Dillon. He showed genuine interest in and concern for his constituents, especially tenant farmers, and despite the consequences, he stoutly defended the freedom of the press. He acted as a conduit from the rarefied halls of Westminster to his readers at home, explaining the workings of parliament, and any new legislation which would affect them. He was sometimes looked upon as a type of teacher by those who depended on newspapers or political meetings for their knowledge of politics. He was a firm believer in the party, and remained convinced that constitutional agitation would eventually succeed in securing home rule, the long-standing priority of the party.

McHugh was just one member of the party which was derided by those who succeeded them as the representatives of Irish nationalist aspirations. By the time they gained the concession of home rule, the political landscape had changed, but their presence at Westminster ensured that Irish matters were not completely ignored by successive governments. Several measures were introduced which attempted to address economic problems in Ireland; local government was democratised, and the land question was finally solved. In October 1916, a statue of McHugh was unveiled in Sligo, and today it stands beside the town hall where he began his political life. By the time it was unveiled, the legacy of the party he loved was being overtaken by a new Irish nationalist movement.

# Notes

ABBREVIATIONS

| | |
|---|---|
| CBS | Crime Branch Special |
| *IHS* | *Irish Historical Studies* |
| NA | National Archives |
| NLI | National Library of Ireland |
| *SC* | *Sligo Champion* |
| *SF* | *Sinn Féin* |
| *UI* | *United Ireland* |
| UIL | United Irish League |

INTRODUCTION

1 Conor Cruise O'Brien, *Parnell and his party, 1880–90* (London, 1968, originally published Oxford, 1957); F.S.L. Lyons, *The Irish parliamentary party, 1890–1910* (Connecticut, 1975, originally published London, 1951).
2 Frank Callanan, *T.M. Healy* (Cork, 1996); J.V. O'Brien, *William O'Brien and the course of Irish politics, 1881–1918* (Los Angeles, 1976); Sally Warwick-Haller, *William O'Brien and the Irish land war* (Dublin, 1990); Denis Gwynn, *The life of John Redmond* (London, 1932).
3 Conor Cruise O'Brien (ed.), *The shaping of modern Ireland* (London, 1960), p. 1.
4 Michael Davitt, *The fall of feudalism in Ireland* (London and New York, 1904), p. 701.
5 Marie-Louise Legg, *Newspapers and Nationalism: The Irish provincial press 1850–1892* (Dublin, 1998).

THE MAKING OF A LOCAL POLITICIAN

1 Although biographical details scarce, the accounts that are available give McHugh's date of birth as September 1858; (Stenson & Lees (eds), *Who's who of British members of parliament Vol. 2 1886–1914* (Sussex, 1976), and Dod, *Parliamentary companion*, published annually; the Roman Catholic register for the parish of Cloonclare records his baptism on 16 March 1859; NLI, microfilm, P 7505.
2 R. Griffith, *Primary valuation of tenements*, County Leitrim 1857, Union of Manorhamilton, Parish of Cloonclare, Barony of Drumahair; *Return of the owners of land of one acre and upwards in the several counties, counties of cities and counties of towns in Ireland*, (reprinted Baltimore, U.S.A., 1988), p. 395.
3 Philip O'Connell, *Schools and scholars of Breifne* (Dublin, 1942), p. 463.
4 O'Connell, *Schools and scholars*, p. 465.
5 *Census of Ireland 1881, Vol. IV province of Connaught*, HC 1882 [c. 3268] lxxix 647.
6 St Patrick's College Archives, Bishop's House, Cullies, Cavan.
7 F.S.L. Lyons, *Charles Stewart Parnell* (London, 1978, originally published 1977), p. 134.

8 Samuel Clark, *The social origins of the Irish land war* (Princeton, 1979), pp 309–26; see also Paul Bew, *Land and the national question in Ireland 1858–82* (Dublin, 1978).
9 Registry of Marriages, Sligo, 3 Nov. 1880.
10 Quoted in John Coolahan, *Irish education: history and structure* (Dublin, 1981), p. 69.
11 For a brief history of Sligo town, see Mary O'Dowd, 'Sligo', in Anngret Simms and J.H. Andrews (eds), *Irish country towns* (Cork, 1994), pp 142–53.
12 *Census of Ireland 1881 Vol. IV Connaught* H.C. [c. 3268] lxxix 534.
13 W.G. Wood-Martin, *A history of Sligo county and town* (3 vols, Dublin, 1882, 1889, 1892), iii, pp 126–90.
14 S. Maxwell-Hajducki, *A railway atlas of Ireland* (Devon, 1974), pp 6, 12.
15 Quoted in R.F. Foster, *W.B. Yeats: a life: i the apprentice mage* (Oxford, 1997), p. 20.
16 John C. McTernan, *Olde Sligoe: aspects of town and county over 750 years* (Sligo, 1995), pp 285–8.
17 Terence O'Rorke, *The history of Sligo town and county* (2 vols, Dublin, 1886), ii, p. 545.
18 *Return of the number of newspaper stamps at one penny issued to newspapers in England, Ireland, Scotland and Wales for the years 1851, 1852, 1853, specifying each Newspaper by name, and the Years to each Newspapers. Number of stamps issued to each of the above.* H.C. (117) 1854 xxxix 479.
19 *SC* 4 Dec. 1880.
20 *SC* 3 July 1880.
21 *SC* 14 Feb. 1884.
22 O'Rorke, *History of Sligo*, ii, p. 547.
23 O'Rorke, *History of Sligo*, ii, p. 549.
24 *SC* 25 July 1885.
25 C.C. O'Brien, *Parnell*, pp 126–33.
26 Brian M. Walker, *Parliamentary election results in Ireland 1801–1918* (Dublin, 1978), p. 312.
27 C.C. O'Brien, *Parnell*, p. 26, n. 2.
28 *SC* 25 Apr. 1885.
29 *SC* 4 Dec. 1880; 13 June 1885; 17 Apr. 1886.
30 *SC* 22 Aug. 1885; 10 Oct. 1885.
31 *SC* 31 Oct. 1885.
32 Virginia Crossman, *Local government in 19th century Ireland* (Belfast, 1994), pp 77–79.
33 Wood-Martin, *A history of Sligo county and town*, iii, p. 111.
34 *SC* 4 Dec. 1888.
35 Mary Daly, *The buffer state: the historical roots of the department of the environment* (Dublin, 1997), p. 13.
36 W.L. Feingold, *The revolt of the tenantry: the transformation of local government in Ireland 1872–86* (Boston, 1984), p. 19.
37 *SC* 23 Oct. 1886.
38 *SC* 27 Feb. 1886.
39 *SC* 12 June 1886.
40 *SC* 13 Feb. 1886; 12 June 1886.
41 *SC* 10 Apr. 1886; 17 Apr. 1886.
42 *SC* 12 June 1886.
43 F.S.L. Lyons, *Charles Stewart Parnell*, p. 345.
44 *SC* 12 June 1886.
45 *SC* 18 Sept. 1886.
46 Committee and membership list of Sligo branch of the Irish National League, 1885, Sligo County Library, 1123 F.C./D.4/5.
47 *SC* 4 Dec. 1880; *Slater's commercial directory of Ireland* (Dublin, 1881).
48 Samuel Clark, 'The social composition of the land league' in *IHS*, xvii, no. 68, (September, 1971), pp 447–69.
49 *SC* 22 Aug. 1885; 16 Jan. 1886.
50 *SC* 10 Apr. 1886.
51 *SC* 12 Sept. 1886.
52 *SC* 2 Jan. 1886; 16 Jan. 1886.
53 48 &49 Vict. c.23; 48 Vict. c.3.
54 Brian M. Walker, 'The Irish electorate 1868–1915', in *IHS*, xviii, no. 71, (March, 1973), pp 359–406, p. 391.
55 *SC* Sept. 1885.

56 *SC* 17 Oct. 1885.
57 *SC* 24 Oct 1885.
58 *SC* Sesquicentnary issue 1986, p. 49; the first was Edward Dwyer Gray MP, proprietor of the *Freeman's Journal*.
59 *SC* 31 Oct. 1885.
60 *SC* 28 Nov. 1885.
61 Walker, *Parliamentary election results*, pp 372–3.
62 *Return of all Charges made to candidates at the late election by Returning Officers, specifying in each case the Numbers of Members returned, and in each case of Contest, the Number of Candidates; also the Total Expenses of each Candidate, both exclusive and inclusive of Returning Officers' Charges, delivered to the Returning Officer pursuant to Corrupt Practices Acts and the number of Votes polled for each candidate*, H.C. 1880 (382–sess.2) lviii 43.
63 *SC* 24 Apr. 1886.
64 *SC* 22 May 1886.
65 *SC* 14 Aug. 1886.
66 *UI* 24 Sept. 1881; SC 1885/86.
67 *Slater's commercial directory 1892* (Dublin, 1892); *Sligo Independent county directory, almanac and guide* (Sligo, 1889).
68 *UI* 24 Sept. 1881; John C. McTernan, *Here's to their memory, profiles of distinguished Sligonians of bygone days* (Cork, 1977), pp 173–76.
69 *UI* 11 Aug. 1883.
70 McTernan, *Here's to their memory*, pp 397–401.
71 *SC* 19 Mar. 1887.
72 *SC* 18 Aug. & 17 Oct. 1885.
73 *SC* 24 Oct & 8 May 1885.
74 *SC* 16 Oct. 1886.
75 *SC* 23 Oct. 1886.
76 *SC* 27 Nov. 1886.
77 Warwick-Haller, *William O'Brien and the Irish land war*, p. 86.
78 *SC* 27 Nov. 1886.
79 *SC* 4 Dec. 1886.
80 *SC* 25 Dec. 1886.
81 *SC* 18 Dec. 1886.
82 *SC* 22 Jan. & 29 Jan. 1887.
83 50 & 51 Vict. c. 20; Virginia Crossman, *Politics, law and order in nineteenth century Ireland* (Dublin, 1996), pp 226–7.
84 *Return of the districts Proclaimed under 'The Criminal Law and Procedure (Ireland) Act 1887' showing the portions of the Act so put in force in each Proclaimed District and the date of the Proclamations*, H.C. 1887 (251) lxvii 525.
85 *SC* 13 Aug. 1887.
86 *SC* 15 Oct.; 29 Oct. 1887.
87 *SC* 3 Dec. 1887.

TOWARDS A WIDER STAGE

1 *SC* 7 Jan. 1888.
2 *SC* 24 Mar. 1888.
3 *SC* 19 May; 28 Apr. 1888.
4 *SC* 17 Mar. 1888.
5 *SC* 7 Apr. 1888.
6 *SC* 28 Apr. 1888.
7 Quoted in Emmet Larkin, *The Roman Catholic church and the plan of campaign*, (Cork, 1978), p. 202.
8 *SC* 5 May 1888.
9 *SC* 12 May 1888.
10 Quoted in Larkin, *The Roman Catholic church*, p. 224.
11 *SC* 26 June 1888.
12 *SC* 2 June 1888.
13 O'Brien, *Parnell*, p. 22–3.
14 *SC* 9 June 1888.
15 *SC* 16 June 1888.
16 *UI* 30 June 1888.
17 *SC* 24 July 1888.
18 *SC* 24 July 1888.
19 *SC* 4 Aug. 1888.
20 *SC* 7 July 1888.
21 T Harrington, *A diary of coercion* (3 vols, Dublin, 1888), ii, p. 106.
22 *SC* 4 Aug. 1888.
23 *SC* 18 Aug. 1888.
24 *SC* 17 Nov. 1888.
25 *Return containing Names of all Persons Proceeded against under the Criminal law and Procedure (Ireland) Act 1887, from Whitsuntide 1888*, to 30 November 1888, H.C. 1889 (28) lxi 479.

26 *SC* 6 Apr. 1889.
27 *SC* 9 Feb. 1889.
28 *SC* 11 May 1889.
29 *SC* 25 May 1889.
30 *SC* 22 June 1889.
31 *SC* 15 June 1889.
32 *SC* 31 Aug. 1889.
33 *SC* 19 Oct. 1889.
34 *SC* 3 Aug. 1889.
35 *SC* 23 Nov. 1889.
36 *SC* 11 Jan. 1890.
37 *SC* 18 Jan. 1890.
38 *SC* 9 Feb. 1890.
39 Quoted in *SC* 25 Jan. 1890.
40 'Political persecution or the history of a broken pledge', in J.J. Clancy, (ed.), *Short lessons on the Irish question or the leaflets of the Irish press agency* (London, 1890), no. 34.
41 L.P. Curtis Jr., *Coercion and conciliation in Ireland 1880–1892, a study in Conservative Unionism* (Princeton, 1963), pp 221–31.
42 *Hansard's parliamentary debates*, 3rd series, vol. 341 col. 744; vol. 342 cols. 694 & 859.
43 *SC* 3 May 1890.
44 *SC* 7 June 1890.
45 *SC* 2 June 1890.
46 N.A., CBS 1482/s 3 Sept. 1890.
47 N.A., CBS 868/s 1890.
48 *SC* 30 Aug. 1890.
49 O'Brien, *Parnell*, p. 287.
50 *SC* 1 Feb. 1890.
51 *SC* 22 Nov. 1890.
52 *SC* 22 Nov. 1890.
53 Quoted in O'Brien, *Parnell*, p. 293.
54 *SC* 29 Nov. 1890.
55 F.S.L. Lyons, *The fall of Parnell* (London, 1962, originally published 1960), p. 326.
56 *SC* 6 Dec. 1890.
57 *SC* 6 Dec. 1890.
58 *SC* 6 Dec. 1890.
59 *SC* 13 Dec. 1890.
60 *SC* 20 Dec. 1890
61 *SC* 20 Dec. 1890.
62 *SC* 27 Dec. 1890.
63 *SC* 7 Feb. 1891.
64 *SC* 14 Feb. 1891.
65 *SC* 14 Mar. 1891.
66 *SC* 21 Mar. 1891.
67 *SC* 28 Mar. 1891.
68 *SC* 28 Mar. 1891.
69 *SC* 18 Apr. 1891.
70 *SC* 18 Apr. 1891.
71 *SC* 4 Apr. 1891.
72 *SC* 4 Apr. 1891.
73 See C.J. Woods, 'The general election of 1892: the catholic clergy and the defeat of the Parnellites', in F.S.L. Lyons and R.A.J. Hawkins (eds), *Ireland under the union: varieties of tension* (Oxford, 1980), pp 289–319.
74 Frank Callanan, *The Parnell split*, (Cork, 1992), pp 113–5.
75 *SC* 4 Apr. 1891.
76 *SC* 11 Apr. 1891.
77 *SC* 16 May 1891.
78 *SC* 16 May 1891.
79 *SC* 13 June 1891.
80 *SC* 18 July 1891.
81 *SC* 18 July 1891.
82 *SC* 10 Oct. 1891.
83 *SC* 28 May 1892.
84 *SC* 28 May 1892.
85 *Leitrim Advertiser* 26 May 1892.
86 *SC* 28 May 1892.
87 *SC* 28 May 1892.
88 Minutes of the Election Committee, 23 Aug; 27 Aug. 1892, J.F.X. O'Brien papers, NLI, MS 5836.
89 *SC* 2 July 1892.
90 Walker, *Parliamentary election results*, p. 359.
91 F.S.L. Lyons, *The Irish parliamentary party 1890–1910*, pp 158–69; the figures refer to Parnellites and anti-Parnellites.
92 *Hansard's Parliamentary Debates*, 4th series, vol. 10, cols. 1414–25.
93 *Hansard*, 4th series, vols 8, 9, 11, 12, 14, 19.
94 *Hansard*, 4th series, vol. 14, col. 340.
95 *Clare Journal*, 22 July 1895.
96 Walker, *Parliamentary election results*, p. 152.

97 *SC* 27 July 1895
98 *SC* 20 July 1895.

TRIALS, OPPORTUNITIES AND CHALLENGES

1 *SC* 11 Jan. 1896.
2 *SC* 6 Nov. 1897.
3 N.A., CBS 15200/s, 1898 committees, Dec. 1897.
4 *SC* 1 Jan. 1898.
5 *SC* 18 Jan. 1898.
6 *SC* 18 Jan. 1898.
7 *Hansard*, 4th series, vol. 53, col. 216.
8 *SC* 26 Feb. 1898.
9 Crossman, *Local government*, pp 91–97; 61 & 61 Vict. c. 37.
10 *Hansard*, 4th series, vol. 53, col. 216.
11 *SC* 6 Aug. 1898.
12 *SC* 23 Apr. 1898.
13 *SC* 28 May 1898.
14 *SC* 20 & 27 Aug. 1898.
15 *SC* 10 Sept. 1898.
16 Warwick-Haller, *William O'Brien*, pp 150–69.
17 *SC* 6 Aug. 1898.
18 *SC* 13 Aug. 1898.
19 *SC* 27 Aug. 1898.
20 William O'Brien's diary, 11 Sept 1898, in the *Irish People*, 16 Feb. 1907.
21 *SC* 24 Sept. 1898.
22 *SC* 8 Oct. 1898.
23 O'Brien's diary, 14 Sept., 2 Oct. 1898, in *Irish People*, 9 Feb., 2 Mar. 1907.
24 N.A., CBS 1725a/s, Origin and history of the U.I.L., 18 Oct. 1898.
25 *SC* 22 Oct. 1898.
26 *SC* 24 Dec. 1898
27 *SC* 14 Jan. 1899.
28 N.A., CBS 18168/s, Elections under the Local Government Act, Dec. 1898.
29 N.A., CBS 18518/s, Forthcoming elections, Feb. 1899.
30 *SC* 4 Feb. 1899.
31 *SC* 25 Feb. 1899.
32 *SC* 18 Feb. 1899.
33 *SC* 11 Mar. 1899.
34 *SC* 25 Mar. 1899.
35 *SC* 8 Apr. 1899.
36 *SC* 29 Apr. 1899.
37 *SC* 5 Aug. 1899.
38 *SC* 16 Sept. 1899.
39 *SC* 23 Dec. 1899.
40 P.J. Bull, 'The reconstruction of the Irish parliamentary party 1895–1903, an analysis with special reference to William O'Brien', unpublished PhD thesis Cambridge University, 1972, pp 203–4.
41 Lyons, *Irish parliamentary party*, p. 89.
42 Paul Bew, *Conflict and conciliation: Parnellites and radical agrarians 1890–1910* (Oxford, 1987), p. 68.
43 *SC* 3 Feb. 1900.
44 *SC* 24 Feb. 1900.
45 Lyons, *The Irish parliamentary party*, pp 149–150.
46 Lyons, *The Irish parliamentary party*, pp 151–52.
47 Lyons, *The Irish parliamentary party*, pp 194–200.
48 Walker, *Parliamentary election results*, p. 161.
49 *SC* 6 Oct. 1900.
50 Philip Bull, 'The United Irish League and the reunion of the Irish parliamentary party 1898–1900', in *IHS* xxvi, no. 101 (May 1988), pp 51–78.
51 *SC* 9 Dec. 1899.
52 *SC* 9 Dec., 16 Dec. 1899, 7 Apr. 1900.
53 *SC* 16 Feb. 1900.
54 *SC* 20 Apr. 1900.
55 *SC* 20 Apr. 1900.
56 *SC* 27 Apr. 1900.
57 N.A., CBS 24930/s, Memos: activities of the UIL etc, 4 July 1901.
58 N.A., CBS 24930/s, Memos: activities of the UIL etc, Chief Secretary to Under Secretary, 24 June 1901.
59 N.A., CBS 24930/s, Memos: activities of the UIL etc, Disturbed areas.
60 N.A., CBS 24930/s, Memos: activities of the UIL, Newspapers which publish intimidatory prosecutions.

61 Dublin City Archives, Minutes of the municipal Council, Dublin 1 Jan.–31 Dec. 1901, p. 603.
62 N.L.I., Redmond papers, Ms 15,203.
63 *SC* 15 Mar. 1902.
64 *SC* 12 Apr. 1902.
65 Philip Bull, *Land, politics and nationalism: a study of the Irish land question* (Dublin, 1996), p. 135.
66 *SC* 12 Apr. 1902.
67 *SC* 2 Aug. 1902
68 *SC* 12 Apr. 1902.
69 *SC* 24 May 1902.
70 *SC* 21 June 1903.
71 *Sligo Nationalist*, 13 Sept. 1903.
72 3 Edw.VII c. 37 (14 Aug. 1903).
73 *SC* 26 Sept. 1903.
74 *SC* 10 Oct. 1903
75 *SC* 22 Aug. 1903.
76 *SC* 7 Nov. 1903
77 Bull, *Land, politics and nationalism*, p. 166.
78 *SC* 9 Jan. 1904.
79 *SC* 27 Feb. 1904.
80 *SC* 8 Apr; 22 July 1904.
81 *SC* 27 Apr. 1907.
82 *SC* 22 June 1907.
83 *SC* 22 June 1907.
84 *SC* 6 July 1907.
85 *SF* 7 July 1907.
86 *SC* 10 Aug. 1907.
87 *SC* 2 Nov. 1907.
88 *SC* 7 Dec. 1907.
89 *SC* 15 Feb. 1908.
90 *SF* 8 Feb. 1908.
91 *SC* 29 Feb. 1908.
92 Ciarán Ó Duibhir, *Sinn Féin the first election 1908* (Manorhamilton, 1993).
93 See Bew, *Conflict and conciliation*; David Seth Jones, *Graziers, land reform and political conflict in Ireland* (Washington, 1995).
94 McTernan, *Olde Sligoe*, pp 496–7.
95 *SC* 12 June 1909.
96 Lyons, *The Irish parliamentary party*, p. 264.